an important life decision about where and how to go to college."

Dr. Ron Strauss
Executive Vice Chancellor and Provost
University of North Carolina at Chapel Hill

"Reflecting on my own college search process that began over 20 years ago, I now realize that my successful matriculation into higher education occurred despite, and not because of, the knowledge I brought to this process. I had a healthy support system; however, as a first-generation college student, I was totally ignorant of the college selection process and like the saying goes, I was unaware that I did not know. I had a gap in my college knowledge that could have jeopardized my ability to get into and be successful in college. Fortunately, I went to an exceptional public high school that had the resources to provide students with college and career counselors who were responsible for helping graduating seniors with their post-secondary planning.

What happens to individuals who lack the knowledge of the college search and are unaware of how to decide if they can thrive at a particular university?

For families who lack an understanding of how to navigate the college search and subsequent choice process, College Roadmap fills this important lack of knowledge base. Providing excellent insight presented in the form of personal stories, "to do" lists, and countless examples, this book is an excellent resource for any family who has students who aspire to higher education. In providing a good blueprint for the selection process College Roadmap can take a complex and sometimes insurmountable process, and present a "how to" in a way that anyone can understand and follow. Perhaps the most unique component of this book is the intentional messaging provided by Dr. Oliver to all the different stakeholders involved in a potential student's sphere of influence during the search process. Dr. Oliver's ability to carve out unique roles and responsibilities for families, students, mentors, and other individuals ultimately confirms the belief held by many that "it takes a village" to assure the success of a college student. Perhaps the most useful resource to readers is the glossary of terms which provides the opportunity for anyone to become a cultural navigator in helping

their students to be successful in college. This is an early must-read for anyone undergoing the college search process."
Dr. Brandon H. Common
Associate Vice President & Dean of Students
Louisiana State University

"This book is a gold mine, especially for first-generation college students and their families!"
Kelly Davidson, M.Ed.
Academic Advisor, Intervention Specialist Education Liaison
Patton College of Education
Ohio University

PRAISE FOR THE SECOND BOOK IN THE ROADMAP SERIES, *CAREER ROADMAP*

"*Career Roadmap* is spot-on from the context of all of the steps that were outlined. In fact, your processes and flow align perfectly to my outline for my upcoming training in this area. I've found that since reviewing *Career Roadmap* and receiving the community work plan, the very things I planned to include as part of my training were included, so I feel confident in volunteering to lead that effort. *Career Roadmap* was my validation and confirmation that I'm on the right track in continuing to help others in the city of Cleveland."

Tia Kline
BBA Mentor
Founder, Equipped4LifeNow
Business Owner and Student Development Professional

"Dr. Greta Oliver has delivered again! *Career Roadmap* is a resource that college students and young professionals can use as they navigate: career exploration, being a job seeker, and changing career paths. She shares stories and vulnerable career moments that made me feel seen, a reminder that we are never alone in our career journey, anxiety, or failures. I see this as a book that folks can keep coming back to as they navigate the rapidly changing working world. Cheers to Dr. O for sharing more of her wisdom and knowledge with us!"

Ashlea Hitchcock-Francis
Founder of THE SQUEEZE

"This book is an authentic example of the real world career or job market. It doesn't make the process of finding a job fluffy and unrealistic. The knowledge in this book will truly prepare the readers for their field of choice. Dr. O asks questions such as 'do you need additional training?' This gives job seekers a real and mature assessment of their skills. *Career Roadmap* allows readers to look at themselves in a reflective way, so that they can take the necessary steps towards improvement as they search for job opportunities that are meaningful to them. Meaningful takeaways were the Holland code and Myers-Briggs personality assessments, both are great self reflection tools that job seekers can use to learn more about themselves for the purposes of finding the career that works for them. There was great detail given to pitch development which is so important to building a brand and taking the readers through the process of thinking of themselves as a brand. This is right in line with today's market. This is also great information if readers are looking to pursue entrepreneurship. Equally important was the discussion regarding the value of mentorship, even including Dr. O's own experience with the SCORE Organization. Mentorship helps the readers get on the right path to clarity regarding their careers earlier versus later. Additionally, the glossary is very helpful, and a wonderful addition to the book."

Dr. Tameka Ellington
Author
Empowerment Speaker
CEO of Dr. Tameka Ellington Enterprises

"There are going to be hurdles when looking for a job, but, if you read Dr. Greta Oliver's book, *Career Roadmap: Setting Yourself Up to Reach Your Career Aspirations*, you will be more prepared for those challenges. This book provides excellent focus and guidance to anyone searching for their dream job. It is full of information that provides you with an action plan for your job search. Dr. Greta Oliver writes her *Career Roadmap* book in a very organized, methodical way; and by reading it, you can start building your career in the same manner. From the first section of the book, *Explore* to the last section *Prevail*, Dr. Oliver provides several assessments, checklists and tips that give you a structured approach to job searching and career success. Well done Dr. Oliver!"

C. Walker, M.A.CCC-SLP
Speech-Language Pathologist

"*Career Roadmap* is an important book that will help many people not only find a way out of an unsatisfying work environment but also help them find a path forward that better utilizes their unique strengths and capabilities. As a senior executive who has worked with too many people in too many companies who come to work each day with a sense of dread or being at a dead end, this book provides not only a way out but a path forward to a more satisfying career. Dr. Oliver doesn't promise magic. You have to do the work. But she provides a concrete, step by step process to help put you on the path to a better and more rewarding life."

Charlie Lehmann
Marketing Consultant and SCORE Mentor

"Throwing a traditional resume at a flurry of job openings doesn't work the way it used to. Getting a great job now requires a different approach. And the keys, as Greta Oliver, PhD, explains clearly in this useful book, are knowing yourself deeply and knowing your ideal employer's needs. *Career Roadmap* pulls together a wealth of resources to provide job seekers with step-by-step instructions to identify work they'll find meaningful, take a detailed inventory of their skills, build a great resume and a network, nail the interview, and get the job. *Career Roadmap* is today's ultimate, practical guide."

Monica Moses
Veteran Writer and Editor

CAREER ROADMAP
SETTING YOURSELF UP TO REACH YOUR CAREER ASPIRATIONS

DR. GRETA OLIVER

DISCLAIMER AND/OR LEGAL NOTICES

While all attempts have been made to verify information provided in this book and its ancillary materials, neither the author nor publisher assumes responsibility for errors, inaccuracies, or omissions and is not responsible for any monetary loss in any matter. If advice concerning legal, financial, accounting, or related matters is needed, the services of a qualified professional should be sought. This book or its associated ancillary materials, including verbal and written training, is not intended for use as a source of legal, financial, or accounting advice. You should be aware of the various laws governing business transactions or other business practices in your state. The information contained in this book is strictly for educational purposes. Therefore, if you wish to apply ideas contained in this book, you are taking full responsibility for your actions. There is no guarantee or promise, expressed or implied, that you will earn any money using the strategies, concepts, techniques, exercises, and ideas in the book.

STANDARD EARNINGS AND INCOME DISCLAIMER

With respect to the reliability, accuracy, timeliness, usefulness, adequacy, completeness, and/or suitability of information provided in this book, Greta Oliver Consulting its partners' associates, affiliates, consultants, and/or presenters make no warranties, guarantees, representations, or claims of any kind. Participants' results will vary depending on many factors. All claims or representations as to income earning are not considered as average earnings. All products and services are for educational and informational purposes only. Check with your accountant, attorney, or professional advisor before acting on this or any information. By continuing with reading this book, you agree that Greta Oliver Consulting is not responsible for the success or failure of your personal, business, or financial decisions relating to any information.

PRINTED IN THE UNITED STATES OF AMERICA | FIRST EDITION
© All Rights Reserved. Copyright 2023. GRETA OLIVER CONSULTING
All rights reserved. No part of this book may be reproduced in whole or part, or stored in a retrieval system, or transmitted in any form or by any means, electronic, mechanical, photocopying, recording, or otherwise, without the written permission of the author.
ISBN 978-1-7375089-2-2 (paperback[b])
ISBN 978-1-7375089-3-9 (Ebook)
Library of Congress Control Number: 2023900947
Printed in Chapel Hill, North Carolina, USA by Greta Oliver Consulting
This book is not intended for use as a source of legal, medical, accounting, or financial advice. All readers are advised to seek the services of competent professionals in the legal, medical, accounting, and financial fields.
The advice and strategies found within may not be suitable for every situation. This work is sold with the understanding that neither the author nor the publisher is held responsible for the results accrued from the advice in this book. Use of this book does not establish any type of advisory, coaching, counseling, or professional relationship with the author or publisher.
For bulk book orders, email Drgreta@gretaoliverconsulting.com
Photo Credits - Envato, Book design, cover designer, graphic illustration, Brittany Annis
For more information, visit www.GretaOliverConsulting.com.

Dedicated with thanks and sincere gratitude to the memory of my first cheerleader, my advocate and the greatest woman I have ever known, my mother, Denola Thomas and to my father, James Thomas who took me to my first job.

"You can only become truly accomplished at something you love. Don't make money your goal. Instead, pursue the things you love doing and then do them so well that people can't take their eyes off you."

MAYA ANGELOU

ACKNOWLEDGMENTS

Many individuals helped with the development of this book which has been created to guide the steps for those in search of their career. I know the book is important because many of my friends and acquaintances are in the process of navigating the daunting task of searching for a career that allows them to fulfill their purpose in life. In today's uncertain world you may find yourselves reinventing yourself and exploring potential careers multiple times. Here are some tools to help you in completing this task logically to enable you to find your true career rather than just a job. Individuals who contributed to this effort:

Brittany Annis
Editor, Designer and Illustrator
Shanghai, China

Michael Gawlik
Website Developer, Content Creator
Simply Told Design
Chapel Hill, North Carolina

Darrel G. Greene Jr.
Website Developer, Content Creator
Holy Mattress Money, CEO
Northfield, Ohio

Terence Oliver
Full Professor, UNC Hussman School of Journalism and Media
University of North Carolina at Chapel Hill
Simply Told Design, CEO
Complex Stories, Motion Graphics Producer
Chapel Hill, North Carolina

Beta Readers:
Dr. Tameka Ellington
Ashley Hitchock-Francis
Tia Kline
Charlie Lehmann
Monica Moses
C. Walker

Career Roadmap Launch Team

SPECIAL ACKNOWLEDGMENT

A special thank you to Juliet Jones-Vlasceanu, GCDF, J.D., President & CEO, Career Key, Inc. Interestingly enough I met Juliet through LinkedIn as I searched for connections that were like-minded, interesting, doing wonderful things and making a difference. I reached out by connecting and forming a relationship and Juliet was so kind to write the foreword to this book. When I say LinkedIn is important for networking and making connections, I really mean it. As you navigate your career search be sure to take advantage of the site because it can certainly help you as it did me.

For over 25 years, Juliet has helped people navigate complex and intimidating systems in the world of work with greater confidence. In over 10 years as a labor and employment lawyer, she advised both sides of the employment relationship: individuals, unions, and managers. She continues to volunteer at her neighborhood legal clinic advising on landlord/tenant, elder, family and criminal record questions. In 2006, Juliet joined Career Key, founded by her father and nationally recognized counseling psychologist and counselor educator, Dr. Lawrence K. Jones, NCC, Professor Emeritus, College of Education at N.C. State University. In 2014, she became CEO and helped lead its transformation into a career well-being and education technology company, nationally certified as a woman-owned business by the Women's Business Enterprise Council. Juliet is a Global Career Development Facilitator (GCDF) and a graduate of Princeton University and the Seattle University School of Law.

CONTENTS

- **FOREWORD**
- **FIRST THINGS FIRST – IS THIS THE BOOK FOR YOU?**
- **PREFACE**
- **MY START, MY STORY**
- **INTRODUCTION**
  - **MY REALITY, ACKNOWLEDGING AND FACING CHANGE**
  - **STEPS TO FINDING YOUR CAREER**

PART 1   EXPLORE - Using Assessments to Determine Your Interests *14*

Holland Codes *15*
    Finding Your Holland Code
    RIASEC Careers List

Myers Briggs Personality Assessment *21*
    Jobs Per Interests

The Three Types of Skills *28*
    Transferable Skills Checklist Assessment
    Determining Your Transferable Skills

PART 2   DEVELOP -Setting Goals for Your Future Career *36*

SMART Goal Setting *39*

Goal Setting Example *40*

Staying On Course *42*

Identifying Your Top Five Values *43*

CliftonStrengths Assessment 44

CliftonStrengths Themes 44

Developing Your Brand 47

PART 3   **PREPARE** 52

Resume Building 54
- Types of Resumes
- Developing Your Resume
- Branding Statement
- Summary Profile

Applicant Tracking Systems 58

Developing Your Elevator Pitch 59

Networking 66
- How to Network
- Where to Network
- Networking on LinkedIn

Organizing Your Networking and Job Search 69

Setting Up Your Job Search Tracking System 70
- Daily Plan Preparation
- Monthly Plan Preparation

Filling Out Applications 72

Interviewing 72

Types of Interviews
Describing Yourself
Preparing for the Interview Process

PART 4 PRESENT 78

Preparing Your Interview Attire 84

Following Up After the Interview 85

Finding a Mentor 85

Joining Professional Organizations 86

PART 5 PREVAIL 88

The Job Offer 90

Negotiation Skills 91

Showing Up Authentically 92

Workplace Etiquette 92

- ■ CONCLUSION
- ■ GLOSSARY
- ■ ABOUT THE AUTHOR
- ■ WORKING PAPERS
- ■ REFERENCES

Foreword
Juliet Jones-Vlasceanu, GCDF, J.D.

As you begin or make a fresh start on your journey to discover a fulfilling and successful career, it can be challenging to navigate a rapidly changing job market and choose from many career pathways. Understanding your interests, values, and skills is crucial in making informed decisions about your career. In her new book *Career Roadmap*, successful author and career advice expert, Dr. Greta Oliver aims to empower you to do just that.

In this helpful guide of essential career development topics, you will actively explore your interests, values, and skills, and learn how to use them to guide your career decisions. You will also learn how to develop a personal brand and communicate effectively in networking and the job search. Dr. Oliver shares her inspiring personal story of career exploration and resilience in the face of change, motivating you to take control of your own career journey.

One of the key concepts this book draws on is Dr. John Holland's theory of vocational choice. As a leading authority on this theory and its application, my company Career Key believes - along with Dr. Oliver - that it provides an excellent foundation for exploring one's personality and interests. Decades of research support it. This practical theory says that individuals are more likely to be satisfied and successful in careers and education programs that align with their personality types. In other words, "birds of a feather flock together."

Holland's theory identifies six personality types sometimes referred to as "Holland Codes." They are, Realistic, Investigative, Artistic, Social, Enterprising and Conventional. This book introduces you to identifying your strongest personality types and matching them with suitable career options. As you take assessments, it's important to use those that are scientifically valid (backed by transparent, significant research) to ensure you get accurate scores and consider the right best-fit careers.

In addition to exploring your unique interests, skills and strengths, in *Career Roadmap* you will also discover the power of networking and learn how to create a personal brand that will help you stand out in the job market. Dr. Oliver provides engaging, practical strategies for building a professional network and shares insights and advice from industry experts and successful professionals.

Networking is not only important for finding job opportunities but also for gaining insights and learning about different industries. You will get a chance to connect with people who can support and mentor you in your career journey. I found this true for myself – my first jobs in law and then after I was laid off in an economic downturn came from networking activities.

In addition to helping you get the most out of networking, Dr. Oliver brings decades of experience with students and job seekers to help you develop a personal brand. She offers practical tips and strategies for applying your personal brand to LinkedIn profiles and resumes. You will learn how to create a resume that will catch the attention of potential employers, survive automated application management systems, strengthen your job search and job applications. In a competitive job market, it's important to have a resume that stands out and effectively showcases who you are, what makes you uniquely qualified to solve the employer's "problem" your target position seeks to solve.

Career Roadmap is an engaging, comprehensive – but not overwhelming - resource that will empower you to understand yourself, set goals, and tackle the job market. Whether you're a recent graduate, a mid-career professional, or someone looking to make a change, this book will equip you with the knowledge and tools you need to take control of your career and achieve success. Start reading now and let Dr. Oliver guide you on your journey to a fulfilling and successful career! With such authentic, informed guidance and inspiration, you will have the knowledge and tools needed to make informed decisions and achieve your career goals.

First Things First – Is This Book For You?

This book is meant to be a resource for individuals who want to make a shift from their current job to another more fulfilling position. Before purchasing this book and getting into how this shift can be made, you might consider the following questions: Are you dissatisfied with where you are and feel like there is more for you? Do you feel like you need to make a change from a job to finding your purpose in life? Do you feel stuck in your current position? Do you desire more satisfaction from your job? If the answer to any of the above questions is "yes," then this is the book for you. The audience for this book is likely a more mature or seasoned employee who feels compelled to make a dramatic change and who is willing to do the work that is required to make the change they desire. This book, while portions of it can be used by anyone who is seeking a job, is best suited for someone who has a good deal of job experience and individuals who have had some successes in their past experiences that they can draw from to move to a more fulfilling position based on their past accomplishments.

This book, *Career Roadmap*, is able to be utilized by the job seeker individually and can also be utilized as a part of my on-demand course, "Career Roadmap: In it to Win It." If you choose to work through the book on your own, you have everything you need right now. If you want to take advantage of the on-demand course, you will need the book which is required. In addition, go to my website, gretaoliverconsulting.com to purchase the on-demand course. In either case, if you have any questions, please feel free to contact me at drgreta@gretaoliverconsulting.com for help.

Preface

If you are like most people on the planet you will have to work at some time or another in your life. In my case I was born into a small family consisting of my parents and one older sibling. We were not wealthy but working middle class, at least in my mind. When I was small my mother did not work but started working right before I went to kindergarten. Surprisingly I can remember this occurrence. Initially my mother's first job was working in a hospital in the dietary department and my father worked at a tire company. Later both of my parents worked in factories in Cleveland and did so until their retirement. At one point during my early childhood I remember my father losing his job at the tire company and having to seek another. Both of my parents worked full time jobs to put food on the table and to maintain our household. There was no thought in either of their minds to pursue a specific career, to make a particular vocation their life's work just because of their passion for that particular field of work. They worked the jobs that they could obtain and did so gladly.

Once I'd gone to college in the pursuit of being a teacher I believed that I'd found my focus. I taught high school immediately after graduation as a business teacher and then went on to work as an accounting clerk in an accounting firm. I eventually changed from teaching because the courses I taught were dwindling in popularity and there were changes being made in the school's curriculum that caused my courses to begin to be offered as electives which became a very slippery slope for me. Initially, I thought I would be an educator forever, but after my first four years of teaching I pursued other jobs in order to have money to contribute to my family. Some of these employment opportunities were simply jobs, while other positions supported my original purpose of working with students. During this time, I still had not found a career that I was content with. Working in sales and as an administrative assistant let me know what I didn't want to do and pushed me to continue searching for purpose. I didn't just want to work a job, I wanted career satisfaction. In taking stock of what I was doing I learned quite a few things that helped to narrow my focus. I found that I was interested in helping others, students primarily; and I was thrilled to think that I could in some way help someone else live a more fulfilling life. I knew I wanted to concentrate on education of some sort. I enjoyed corporate training and being a student advocate and college administrator. I've always enjoyed reading and thought I would take a risk and write about the things I love doing based on my experience and education. I like being a coach to others because it encompasses the best of everything I love and provides me with the opportunity to share that knowledge with others.

So that's my story based on my passion and I'm working toward making it my career. This is exactly what I hope you will do. Start by evaluating the things you love, take assessments and even ask people what they think you would be good at. Seek out new things but don't forget about your old experiences. Look back on your past experiences as learning opportunities and use everything. I don't believe that anything is wasted. Take what you have learned and insert the good of those experiences into your future, evaluate and discard the negative and make an effort not to repeat negative experiences. Determine the things that you like and the things that are deal breakers. Find out what you are passionate about and explore how you can use those things to provide a service to others. Evaluate your strengths and develop your skill set. Set goals along the way to keep you focused and pursue your dream!

The bottom line is this, since we spend so much of our lives "working" it would be such a blessing to be able to spend your time "working" in a place you love, fulfilling your life purpose and finding satisfaction in doing so. I am hoping that if you are reading this book about finding a career that you love and pursuing your dreams and purpose relative to your passions, you will press on to find a career that you love which allows you to provide a service that you would do even if you were not being paid.

My Start, My Story

To be honest, I have a lot of experience in searching for a job and/or career. Not all of it is good. Let's start at the beginning. As I mentioned elsewhere in the book, my first job was working the summer after I graduated from high school in a factory. I worked that job each summer while I was in college. Working this grueling factory job certainly let me know that I wasn't cut out for factory work and that standing on concrete floors for hours on end doing physical labor was not for me. College never looked so good!

During college I worked several jobs on campus in various offices and in the library and also for university catering. I did not have to work, but chose to. These jobs were not pieces of cake either and for the most part were just a means to an end and allowed me to have some money of my own while I was a college student that didn't come from home. From these jobs I learned a great deal about where I did not want to work and what type of job was more comfortable for me.

When I went to college I majored in business education. I wanted to be a business teacher and I did just that, but even with a degree in hand, obtaining my first teaching job was not easy. I went on various interviews with a few of the larger districts near my home town of Cleveland, Ohio but did not have any offers. I eventually landed a job teaching for the lowest paying Catholic School in America, maybe even on the planet. I had six large classes and received a minuscule paycheck, once a month and nothing in the summer. This was supposed to be my career? I'd wanted to be a business teacher since the 7th grade, and I was being paid less than minimum wage! This didn't seem fair or right when I compared myself to my peers who had gone to college and even to those who had not. I stayed at this particular school for two years and then left.

Next, I worked at an accounting firm and, although I made more money than I did as a teacher, I later found out that I was not being paid fairly. This was a national accounting firm that had posted salary scales and the whole nine yards. Years later I found out I was paid below the salary scale during my time there, I lasted a year. Following that job I went back to teaching again but at yet another parochial school. The pay was almost double, but still low, and I was there for four years. Many temporary jobs followed, then I entered into the world of corporate training where I stayed for about 7 years. After a corporate buyout, I eventually returned to teaching where not only was I paid well, but also treated fairly in a career that I actually loved.

It is not my plan to tell you about every job I've had, but rather that, regardless of what I did, I always returned to my first love, which was teaching students, both young and old. Over the years, I trained or taught at various schools and colleges on every academic level and in different capacities. Now I can see that teaching students has truly been my career!

When I retired from teaching I decided to continue my connection with students by writing a book that was specifically for them. *College Roadmap* was born. Continuing in that vein, I decided to write another book in the *Roadmap* series. *Career Roadmap* is a guide for those who want to focus on finding their true calling in life, doing something that they love.

In this book I am focusing on career development for the most part even though I realize that people have different trajectories to their true career path. Just like my road was winding, with various stops and starts, many others have had this same experience. The truth is, it can be hard to find your career path and sometimes you will make mistakes or missteps along the way. Basically, the traditional way of finding a job is fraught with problems. The new normal and fastest method of gaining employment is through networking and personal branding. Presently, as an entrepreneur I make connections with people when promoting my book and services by pointing out how by buying my book or utilizing my services, clients can be in a better place or a problem that they have can be solved. The employment search is no different. In order for a person who is searching for their career or job to move forward they have to be the answer to their prospective hiring manager's problem. That's where personal branding, knowing who you are, knowing your skills and knowing your worth comes in. We will talk about exploring and getting to know yourself and your interests, skills, values, and abilities and then how to utilize what you know about yourself to develop a brand for yourself to become someone an employer can't resist hiring. Why, because of your confidence, skills and track record, you represent an answer to their problems. We will develop you as a person who can meet the needs of the employer for whom you wish to work. We will also talk about practical things that can help prepare you as well during your search such as employment documents, proper attire, etiquette, organization, and authenticity. All of these topics will help you to be able to present yourself as a successful employee who is able to prevail and come out on top in a career that you love.

Introduction

Job versus career? In general a job is a means to making money. While a career is a position that is held and is typically characterized as a way of making money that is coupled with a love or passion for that particular line of work. In essence the term career is a bit broader and while both are ways of receiving income, a career that you are very passionate about pursuing is something that you would do if money didn't even come into play. For the purposes of this book, though, I will use the terms job and career interchangeably. What I really want is for you to find your passion and begin working in an area where you would do it for free because the work is a part of your purpose, what you were meant to do and why you are here. Sometimes it will take a while to determine your purpose and to become immersed in a career that supports your purpose but it can be achieved as you press toward fulfilling your life goals. Whether or not you went to college, there will come a time in your life when you will be searching for a job or career. In fact, studies have shown that on average, people will change their jobs or careers approximately 12 times in their lifetime (Kolmar, 2022). This job changing trend is even more prevalent for Millennials and Gen Z-ers. According to Zippia (2022), on average, a millennial will stay at their job for 2.75 years. According to a Gallup report on the millennial generation, 21% of Millennials surveyed report changing jobs within the past year – more than three times the rate of other generations. Gen Z-ers are switching jobs at a rate 134% higher than before the pandemic in 2019, according to LinkedIn. Comparatively, Millennials changed jobs 24% more, and boomers switched 4% less. Gen Z is more likely to work multiple jobs (25%) than the average professional (16%), according to McKinsey as cited in Vemparala, (2022). Because a person will most likely experience so many changes regarding their life's work, it is important to have strategies in place for the process to be as easy as possible. This book can be an outline for you to use as you go through the process of pursuing your career.

 ROADSIDE NOTES

My Reality: Acknowledging and Facing Change

Sometimes I feel like a fraud when giving advice about job searching and careers because honestly, I have faced great difficulty in this area over the years. As it happens, I now believe that a great deal of the struggle I experienced was a result of both a broken system and poor timing. However, it was hard to see it from that perspective while I was in the midst of the chaos. They say that hindsight is 20-20, and now looking back I do believe that statement to be true. Let me explain. You know about my early experiences in securing a job in education, but what you may not know are the details of what I experienced later in my career, when I left Ohio and moved to North Carolina. Initially when my husband and I made the move down South, I was exhilarated about the possibility of continuing to work in higher education in a new, warmer state that was the home of many educational institutions--that I was sure was just waiting for someone like me to appear. Working with students was my life's greatest joy and I wanted to continue working in what I believed was my purpose. When I arrived in North Carolina, I had a rude awakening. While I was correct that there were many educational institutions, it was also true that there were many other people who had a similar background, education and amount of work experience as I did. There were also more PhDs per capita than perhaps anywhere else in the country. Ultimately, my credentials didn't mean much. I updated my resume, told everyone I knew that I was searching for a position, submitted application after application, and I waited. I landed a few interviews and even second interviews, but no dream job offers materialized. This caused me to begin to doubt myself and my ability. The positions I eventually would take on were not because of my top notch credentials, terminal degree, or many years of experience in all levels of education. They were solely the result of networking. Every position I was offered was a direct result of connections I'd made with good people including family and friends, who had spread the word about my background and availability. During this time, I worked primarily at a university in an interim, full-time, albeit limited position, and also held two part-time positions. Additionally, I worked at a community college part time for several years teaching employability skills like those found in this book, and rewriting curriculum for the same department. Based on what I experienced and the experiences of others, I know for a fact that the traditional way of job hunting that has been in place forever no longer works for everyone. It did not work for me but because it did not work, I suffered damaging blows to my self esteem and self worth. I now realize that this was not a failure on my part. Additionally, I realized that since the old way did not work, a new approach was needed in order to positively impact the process of job hunting. Job hunters now have to embrace the new and make changes in our methodology in order to be successful. If you're doing everything "right" and still struggling to advance your career, it's time to take the blame off of yourself! It's not your fault! Throw away the list of excuses and get to work, pun intended. Start by getting to know yourself, what you want to do, and who you want to be. Develop and hone your skills for the position you desire, build up your confidence, establish your brand, and develop your elevator pitch to be able to clearly articulate how you can make a lasting difference that will directly and positively impact your prospective employer with cold, hard, facts! Position yourself as the answer, the problem solver, and the clear and only choice. It's time to get your "yes" and move forward into the life that you want to live.

Steps to Finding Your Career

Not knowing what you need to know is a big mistake when pursuing your career. Knowledge is power. Your success depends upon what you know. So one of the very first things you should know is yourself. What do you have to offer the world? What abilities and skills do you possess? What areas need improvement in your life? Next, what are your strengths and weaknesses? What are your interests? What are your values and what do you value? Is there a career that stands out for you? What is your purpose in life? How easily are you able to learn new things or adapt to new surroundings? The answers to all of these questions and many more are important to your success as you move forward in search of a career that fits.

Step 1 - Know Yourself and What You Want

Self examination is so important. Think about and define the kind of work that you want to obtain. Ask yourself if your choice is something you would do even if you weren't getting paid. Set aside a portion of every day to work on getting a job. Be diligent with this. Remember, you will have to do the work to get where you ultimately want to be. Take an assessment or several to determine the work that you are suited for and then set short and long term SMART goals that are specific to your career. Make sure that you are being realistic in your job choice. Are your goals specific and attainable? Is your objective a targeted one? Can you name the primary type of work or career you are interested in? Do you have adequate experience in the area of your job choice? Do you have any internships or volunteer activities that you can count as experience? If not, are you prepared for future study? Other questions you might ask are:

- What are your salary requirements?
- What benefits do you need?
- What can you picture yourself doing?
- What are you passionate about?
- What does your overall "package" or job offer need to look like?

If your answers to the above questions are already predetermined, you will be able to recognize if a job offer is worth considering.

Step 2 - Determine What You Have to Offer

Complete a skills analysis – what are your skills? You should be able to identify them and communicate how you have made a difference or will make a difference in your new career as a result of the skills you possess. What are your achievements? Make sure you can easily explain exactly what you have done to impact the bottom line of any past employers. Take five minutes to write down every job skill you can bring to your next employer. Ready, set, GO!

MY SKILLS

_____
_____
_____
_____
_____
_____
_____
_____
_____
_____

Take a look at the things you have identified above. Ask yourself these questions relative to each item you listed: Do you have a concrete example of how you performed that shows that what you listed is a valuable offering to an employer? Is it quantifiable? Meaning, can you tie any cost savings, increased productivity or any other gain that was of value to an organization in which you worked to what you listed above? In other words can you prove that the items you listed above were of value to the organization and how? If you can't prove the value of your offerings, you may need to rethink the items on your list.

Step 3 - Know the Job Market

Once you have identified a career path it is important to know as much as possible about the career(s) you are interested in pursuing. You will want to know how the labor market that supports each career operates. You will want to know the specific job functions that are associated with any career you are contemplating. How has that specific career been affected by technological advancements? Is the career viable? Is it growing or is the future of the career questionable? Do you need additional training? If so, find the help you need.

ROADSIDE NOTES

Understand the Viability of Your Career

An example of why it is so important to be sure of the viability of your career over time can be found in my own search for a career. As a junior high student I was introduced to typing in junior high school. You know this was a long time ago since junior high school is not a term that is used anymore, it's now middle school, but I digress. I had a wonderful typing teacher and she was also one of the few teachers that I had that looked like me. I thought the world of this teacher and it didn't hurt that I was very good at typing, excellent in fact. Truthfully, I was probably one of the fastest typists in the class. Because of this experience I decided then and there that I wanted to be a business education teacher. I continued enrolling in business subjects and excelled in them all the way through high school. When I was in high school, there was a requirement that all students had to take at least one semester of typing. That was no problem for me and based on this fact, the idea of a business education teacher as a career choice seemed to be viable. I did not do any further research. I just deduced that since typing teachers were needed and students were required to take typing, the field was a good choice. I left for college and majored in business education with the dreams of becoming a high school business teacher just like my junior high school teacher. Four years later, I was searching for a job as a business education teacher in area high schools around Cleveland. During this time it was hard to find a job for several reasons. The first reason was because of the longevity of teachers in the field. There were not many openings for business education teachers because the teachers in the classrooms had not reached retirement age. The second reason was because many changes were being made in the curricula of the nation's high schools. Courses like typing were no longer requirements that had to be taken by all students. They became electives, meaning that students who wanted to take them could choose to do so and if a student did not choose to take typing, they had no incentive to do so. I eventually found a job at a parochial school and I taught business courses for two years. I taught other business courses as well and enjoyed doing so but the pay was abysmal. I was disheartened. I left teaching and went to work at an accounting firm. I thought I would be happy there because the job was related to business education, and I enjoyed teaching accounting, but this job ended up being a year-long nightmare as I described earlier. Because I did not understand the market and viability for my initial teaching job, I was in a pretty bad position. I was stuck, unfulfilled and still in search of my ultimate career.

Step 4 - Get Your Mind Together

Find your focus and make sure you are ready to take on the job search process. Job searching can be hard. If you take the time to do the work in advance and to find out what you really want and have to offer, it will be worth it. Realize that you will most likely be rejected at some point in the process but don't internalize any rejection. Keep moving forward and use your rejection as a way to propel yourself forward toward a career/job that you will absolutely love. Endeavor to identify and learn from your mistakes. Make a real effort to do your very best. Don't give up!

In this book you will find many assessments. The assessments are a guide to help you figure out many things about yourself and your possible interests. You might find after filling out a few of them that they may indicate something different than what you expected, that's perfectly fine since the results generated are not guaranteed to be absolutes. While they can be a bit overwhelming they are each important to complete so that you can potentially discover who you are, what you want in a career and the skills that you need to get there. So, if you're ready, let's go!

PART 1
EXPLORE

Using Assessments to Determine Your Interests

Job fit is very important. Since you can expect to spend a great deal of time in your life working, it might be a good idea to determine the types of things you are interested in and passionate about doing. There are many ways to determine your interests. We will discuss several of the ways in this book.

HOLLAND CODES

"When an article written by John L. Holland (1959) entitled, "A Theory of Vocational Choice," was published in the Journal of Counseling Psychology 50 years ago, it is unlikely that many readers would have anticipated the theory's eventual impact" (Nauta, 2010). However the contents of this article were eventually developed into an interest inventory that when completed generates a three letter code describing a person's top interests. Holland's interest inventory, aside from returning a code, also corresponds to lists of jobs or careers that are suited to the interests generated by the assessment. Examination of the codes generated by the Holland Inventory can help inform your search when you are exploring a new position or career. Holland's theory expert Dr. Lawrence K. Jones, describes the importance of the six Holland personality types and their connection to career choice in this way. Choosing a career or education program that fits your Holland personality is a vital step toward career well-being and success–job satisfaction, good grades, and graduating on time. You want to say, "Yes!" to the question, "Do you like what you do each day?" Below are the 6 type descriptors associated with John Holland's research on career fit. In order to determine your three letter type, complete the survey on page 18.

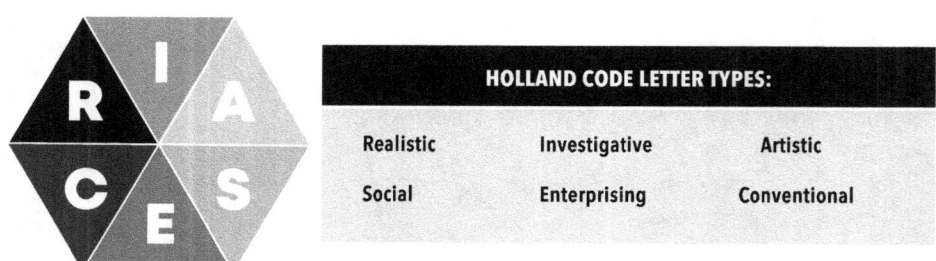

Remember, the Holland Code that is generated for the user is displayed in three letters and represents an individual's three dominant personality types out of six possible choices, according to a theory developed by Dr. John Holland, a psychologist. Descriptions of the six personality types generated by the Holland Code Interest Inventory are as follows:

Realistic
- Likes to work with animals, tools, or machines, or things; generally avoids social activities like teaching, healing, and informing others
- Has good skills in working with tools, mechanical or electrical drawings, machines, or plants and animals
- Values practical things you can see, touch, and use like plants and animals, tools, equipment, or machines
- Sees themselves as practical, mechanical, and realistic.

Example: Auto mechanic

Investigative
- Likes to study and solve math or science problems; generally avoids leading, selling, or persuading people
- Is good at understanding and solving science and math problems
- Values science; and sees themselves as precise, scientific, and intellectual

Example: Rocket scientist

Artistic
- Likes creative activities like art, drama, crafts, dance, music, or creative writing; generally avoids highly ordered or repetitive activities
- Has good artistic abilities -- in creative writing, drama, crafts, music, or art
- Values the creative arts -- like drama, music, art, or the works of creative writers
- Sees themselves as expressive, original, and independent

Example: Concert pianist

Social
- Likes to help people -- interested in teaching, nursing, or giving first aid, providing information; generally avoids using machines, tools, or animals to achieve a goal
- Is good at teaching, counseling, nursing, or giving information
- Values helping people and solving social problems; and is a people person
- Sees themselves as helpful, friendly, and trustworthy

Example: Elementary school teacher

Enterprising
- Likes to lead and persuade others, and to sell things and ideas; generally avoids activities that require careful observation and scientific, analytical thinking
- Is good at leading people and selling things or ideas
- Values success in politics, leadership, or business
- Sees themselves as energetic, ambitious, and sociable

Example: Salesperson

Conventional
- Likes to work with numbers, records, or machines in a set and orderly way; generally avoids ambiguous, unstructured activities
- Is good at working with written records and numbers in a systematic, orderly way
- Values success in business
- Sees themselves as orderly, and good at following a set plan

Example: Accountant

Reprinted with permission from the Career Key website, www.careerkey.org. For more about Holland's Theory and how to use the Holland hexagon, go to www.careerkey.org/fit/personality/hollands-theory-of-career-choice.

Please note, when using the Holland Code Career Assessment, all personality types have both positive and negative qualities and none are better than the others. The Holland Code you receive as a result of completing the assessment is a generalization and not likely to be an exact fit. The following condensed survey is not intended to be as accurate or comprehensive as the full instrument. Completing the survey will help you identify the clusters of occupations in which you may have the most interest and get the most satisfaction, and it will also give you a place to start to focus your career exploration. Once you determine your interests, continue to explore the other assessment instruments in the book for additional results regarding your possible interests, values, and affinities.

Find Your Holland Code

STEP 1
Circle the number of all items that are appealing to you. Leave the others blank.

1. Planting/growing crops
2. Solving math problems
3. Being in a play
4. Studying other cultures
5. Talking to people at a party
6. Working with computers
7. Working on cars/lawn mowers
8. Astronomy
9. Drawing/painting
10. Going to church
11. Working on a sales campaign
12. Using a cash register
13. Carpentry
14. Physics
15. Foreign language
16. Working with youth
17. Buying clothes for a store
18. Working from nine to five
19. Setting type for a printing job
20. Using a chemistry set
21. Reading fiction or plays
22. Helping people with problems
23. Selling life insurance
24. Typing a report
25. Driving a truck
26. Working in a lab
27. Playing a musical instrument
28. Making new friends
29. Leading a group
30. Following a budget
31. Fixing electrical appliances
32. Building rocket models
33. Writing stories or poetry
34. Attending sports events
35. Making your opinions heard
36. Using business machines
37. Building things
38. Doing puzzles
39. Fashion design
40. Belonging to a club
41. Giving talks or speeches
42. Keeping detailed record
43. Wildlife biology
44. Using science to get answers
45. Going to concerts or the theater
46. Working with elderly
47. Sales people
48. Filing letters and reports

STEP 2

On the chart below, circle the number of the items which appeal to you. Then count the number for each row and write the number in the box on the left. The two highest categories are the clusters in which you have the most interest, and their corresponding labels are your Holland Code. (For example, if you scored highest in Social, second highest in Artistic, and third highest in Conventional, your Holland Code would be SAC.) This is where you will focus your career exploration.

Total Line Score

from department of workforce services, jobs.utah.gov

	R = Realistic	1	7	13	19	25	31	37	43
	I = Investigative	2	8	14	20	26	32	38	44
	A = Artistic	3	9	15	21	27	33	39	45
	S = Social	4	10	16	22	28	34	40	46
	E = Enterprising	5	11	17	23	29	35	41	47
	C = Conventional	6	12	18	24	30	36	42	48

Highest Score _____ Second Highest Score _____ Third Highest Score
My Holland Code is _____

STEP 3

Using the 3 highest scores from above look at the careers that are associated with your three letter code using the following charts:

RIASEC Careers List

R

Pilot – Architectural Drafter – Computer Engineer – Conservation Officer Corrections Officer – Diver – Cost Estimator – Firefighter – Forester Mechanical Engineer – Police Officer – Prosthetist/Orthotist – Optician Organic Greenhouse Owner – Military Officer – Electrician – Plumber Film Industry Technician – Remote Operated Vehicle Technician and Operator Construction Worker – Landscape Architect – Civil Engineer – Zookeeper Animal Health Technologist – Zookeeper – Farmer – Carpenter – Jeweler

I

Marine Engineer – Anthropologist – Chiropractor – Computer Programmer
Dentist – Economist – Geographer – Market Research Analyst – Actuary
Meteorologist – Nurse – Pediatrician – Pharmacist – Public Health Inspector
Food Scientist – Medical Microbiologist – Seismologist – Statistician
Translator – Veterinarian – Entomologist – Optometrist – Paleontologist
Safety Engineer – Forensic Accountant – Physician – Management Consultant
Oceanographer – Kinesiologist – Geographic Information Systems Analyst
Non-Destructive Tester – Health Policy Analyst

A

Actor – Advertising Manager – Architect – English Teacher – Fashion Designer
Film Designer – Interior Designer – Journalist – Landscape Architect
Package Designer – Photographer – Set Designer – Screenwriter
Computer Animator – Web Designer – Book Editor – Musician – Copywriter
Museum Curator – Advertising Art Director – Graphic Designer – Librarian
Industrial Designer – Makeup Artist – Radio and Television Announcer
Translator – Film Producer

S

Art Therapist – Cruise Director – Preschool Teacher – Occupational Therapist
Probation Officer – Recreation Therapist – Speech Therapist – Park Naturalist
Midwife – Social Worker – Recruiter – Naturopathic Doctor – Athletic Therapist
Employment Counselor – Family Services Worker – Sign Language Interpreter
Foreign Service Officer – Human Resource Manager – Counseling Psychologist
Volunteer Director – Child Life Therapist – Dental Hygienist – Psychologist
Emergency Medical Technician – Respiratory Therapist – School Counselor

E

Bank Manager – Buyer – Financial Planner – Funeral Home Director
Hotel Manager – Industrial/Organizational Psychologist – Insurance Agent
Lawyer – Production Manager – Real Estate Agent – Retail Store Manager
Stockbroker – Urban Planner – Publisher – Politician – Theater Manager
Newscaster – Reporter – Public Relations Specialist – Travel Agent – Mediator
Appraiser – Event Planner – Detective – Sales Representative – Film Director
Fundraiser – Lobbyist – Quality Control Analyst – School Principal

C

Accountant – Flight Attendant – Building Inspector – Court Reporter
Credit Officer – Customs Inspector – Legal Secretary – Library Assistant
Medical Records Technician – Receptionist – Administrative Assistant
Underwriter – Benefits Analyst – Auditor – Tax Examiner – Collector and Agent
Insurance Adjuster – Air Traffic Controller – Cartographer – Water Inspector
Pharmacy Technician – Computer Security Coordinator

From uManitoba.ca (Note: this list does not contain every job; new roles are developed every day, but the above aptitudes remain applicable.)

Now that you have completed the Holland Assessment, you might want to complete the Myers Briggs Personality Assessment to determine what your personality preference is.

Myers Briggs Personality Assessment

Below are four questions, and descriptions of two lists of personality preferences. Both lists have strengths and weaknesses and both lists are valuable. Neither list is better or worse than the other. Read the lists for Question 1 and decide which list, as a whole, describes you better. Then draw a check mark next to the list that most closely describes you. Answer truthfully. Continue this process with the other three questions. After completing your assessment, write down your four letter code in the space provided at the end of the assessment.

For educational purposes only. This assessment is included for your individual use and not for any profit-making purposes. Retrieved from http://www.personalitytype.com/career_quizPage3

1. Where is your energy naturally directed?
Extroverts' energy is directed primarily outward, toward other people and things. Introverts' energy is primarily directed inward, towards their own thoughts, perceptions, and reactions. Extroverts tend to be more naturally active, expressive, social and interested in many things. On the other hand, introverts tend to be more reserved, private, cautious, and interested in fewer interactions, but with greater depth and focus.

Extroverts often:	Introverts often:
■ Have high energy	■ Have quiet energy
■ Talk more than listen	■ Listen more than talk
■ Think out loud	■ Think quietly inside their own heads
■ Act, then think	■ Think, then act
■ Like to be around other people	■ Feel comfortable being alone
■ Prefer a public role	■ Prefer to work behind the scenes
■ Can sometimes be easily distracted	■ Have good powers of concentration
■ Prefer to do lots of things at once	■ Prefer to focus on one thing at a time
■ Are outgoing and enthusiastic	■ Are self contained and reserved

Choose one:_____ Extrovert (E) or_____ Introvert (I)

2. What kind of information do you naturally notice and remember?

Sensors notice the facts, details and realities of the world whereas intuitives are more interested in connections between facts as well as the meaning of things. Sensors tend to be practical and literal people, who trust past experience and often have good common sense. Intuitives tend to be imaginative, theoretical people who trust their hunches and pride themselves on their creativity.

Sensors often:	Intuitives often:
■ Focus on details and specifics	■ Focus on the big picture and possibilities
■ Admire practical solutions	■ Admire creative ideas
■ Notice details and remember facts	■ Notice anything new and different
■ Are pragmatic - see what is	■ Are inventive - see what could be
■ Live in the here and now	■ Think about future implications
■ Trust actual experience	■ Trust their gut instincts
■ Like to use established skills	■ Prefer to learn new skills
■ Like step by step instructions	■ Like to figure things out
■ Work at a steady pace	■ Work in bursts of energy

Choose one:_____ Sensor (S) or _____ Intuitive (N)

3. How do you decide or come to conclusions?

Thinkers often:
- Make decisions objectively
- Appears cool and reserved
- Are most convinced by rational arguments
- Are honest and direct
- Value honesty and fairness
- Take few things personally
- Are good at seeing flaws
- Are motivated by achievement
- Argue or debate issues for fun

Feelers often:
- Decide based on values and feelings
- Appear warm and friendly
- Are most convinced by their feelings
- Are diplomatic and tactful
- Value harmony and compassion
- Take things personally
- Are quick to compliment others
- Are motivated by appreciation
- Avoid arguments and conflicts

Choose one: _____ Thinker (T)   or   _____ Feeler (F)

4. What kind of environment makes you the most comfortable?

Judgers prefer a structured, ordered, and predictable environment, where they can make decisions. Perceivers prefer to experience as much of the world as possible, so they like to keep their options open and are comfortable adapting. Judgers tend to be organized and productive while perceivers tend to be flexible and nonconforming.

Judgers often:
- Like to have things settled
- Take responsibility seriously
- Pay attention to time; are usually prompt
- Prefer to finish projects
- Work first, play later
- Seek closure
- See the need for most rules
- Like to make and stick with plans
- Find comfort in schedule

Perceivers often:
- Like to keep their options open
- Are playful and casual
- Are less aware of time; may run late
- Prefer to start projects
- Play first, work later
- Struggle to make some decisions
- Question the need for rules
- Like to keep plans flexible
- Want freedom to be spontaneous

Choose one: _____ Judger (J)   or   _____ Perceiver (P)

Now write down your four letter code based upon the choices you made earlier:

_____ _____ _____ _____

Now that you have discovered your Myers Briggs Type, below you will find fields and general categories of careers based upon your Myers Briggs Code. Using the code combination you determined on the assessment above, check the list below to see if you agree with the fields and career categories assigned to an individual with your exact code.

ISTJ

FIELDS	CAREERS
Management	Auditor
Administration	Accountant
Law Enforcement	Chief Financial Officer
Accounting	Web Development Engineer
	Government Employee

ISFJ

FIELDS	CAREERS
Education	Dentist
Healthcare	Elementary School Teacher
Religion	Librarian
	Franchise Owner
	Customer Service Representative

INFJ

FIELDS	CAREERS
Religion	Therapist
Counseling	Mental Health Counselor
Teaching	HR Diversity Manager
Art	Development Consultant
	Customer Relations Manager

INTJ

FIELDS	CAREERS
Science	Investment Banker
Technical Fields	Personal Financial Advisor
Computers	Software Developer
Legal	Economist
	Executive

ISTP

FIELDS	CAREERS
Skilled Trades	Civil Engineer
Technical Fields	Economist
Agriculture	Pilot
Law Enforcement	Data Communications Analyst
Military	Emergency Room Physician

ISFP

FIELDS	CAREERS
Healthcare	Fashion Designer
Business	Physical Therapist
Law Enforcement	Massage Therapist
	Landscape Architect
	Store Keeper

INFP

FIELDS	CAREERS
Counseling	Graphic Designer
Writing	Psychologist/Therapist
Arts	Writer/Editor
	Physical Therapist
	Hr Development Trainer

INTP

FIELDS	CAREERS
Science	Computer Programmer/Software Designer
Technical Fields	Financial Analyst
	Architect
	College Professor
	Economist

ESTP

FIELDS	CAREERS
Marketing	Detective
Skilled Trades	Banker
Business	Investor
Law Enforcement	Entertainment Agent
Applied Technology	Sports Coach

ESFP

FIELDS	CAREERS
Healthcare	Child Welfare Counselor
Teaching	Physician
Coaching	Actor
Skilled Trades	Interior Designer
Childcare	Environment Scientist

ENFP

FIELDS	CAREERS
Counseling	Journalist
Teaching	Advertising Creative Director
Religion	Consultant
Arts	Restaurateur
	Event Planner

ENTP

FIELDS	CAREERS
Science	Entrepreneur
Management	Real Estate Developer
Technology	Advertising Creative Director
Arts	Marketing Director
	Politician/Political Consultant

ESTJ

FIELDS	CAREERS
Management	Insurance Sales Agent
Administration	Pharmacist
Law Enforcement	Lawyer
	Project Manager
	Judge

ESFJ

FIELDS	CAREERS
Education	Sales Representative
Healthcare	Nurse/Healthcare Worker
Religion	Social Worker
	PR Account Executive
	Loan Officer

ENFJ

FIELDS	CAREERS
Religion	Advertising Executive
Arts	Public Relations Specialist
Education	Corporate Coach/Trainer
	Sales Manager
	Employment Specialist
	HR Professional

ENTJ	
FIELDS	**CAREERS**
Management	Executive
Leadership	Lawyer
	Market Research Analyst
	Management Consultant
	Business Consultant
	Venture Capitalist

Source: "Do What You Are: Discover the Perfect Career for You Through the Secrets of Personality Type" by Paul D. Tieger, Barbara Barron, and Kelly Tieger

In general, the information that appears regarding the Myers Briggs Type Code generated includes areas that mesh well with a specific personality type. This information is a lot more general than the information that is associated with a Holland Code. However, these broad categories should give you an indication of areas that may be of interest to you if you have a particular Myers Briggs Code. Examine the careers and interests that were generated by both assessments and determine if any stand out to a greater degree. If you find that there are a few careers that are of interest, conduct additional research to find out more about each particular career. You may also want to check LinkedIn to see if you can find any connections that are working or have worked in the career field you are interested in finding more about. Also use the internet to research those careers. You might also look into professional organizations that are associated with your career field. Go one step further and research the skills and or qualifications that a person in the field might have. Do you have those same skills? If you don't, can you get them? Next, do a skill inventory of your own, using the information below.

The Three Types of Skills

There are three basic types of skills that will be useful in your exploration of finding a career that you love! They are:
- Transferable/Functional Skills
- Knowledge Based/Job-Related Skills
- Personal Trait/Adaptive Skills

TRANSFERABLE/FUNCTIONAL SKILLS

A transferable skill is an ability or expertise which may be used in a variety of roles or occupations, this means you can transfer these skills from job to job. Examples include communication skills, the ability to problem-solve and self-discipline.

KNOWLEDGE BASED/JOB-RELATED SKILLS

These are skills you need to perform a specific job.

PERSONAL TRAITS/ADAPTIVE SKILLS

These are personality traits or personal characteristics. These skills help a person to adapt or get along in a new situation.

You will need to evaluate yourself in each skill area to be sure that you have the skills you need to be successful in your career. If after filling out the assessment below, you find that you are lacking in any skill area, take the time to build your skill base so you will have exactly what you need to pursue and obtain your dream job.

Note: Permission is hereby granted to reproduce the above information for use with clients in career counseling. ©2012 SkillScan

Identifying Your Transferable Skills

Complete the following skills checklist to see where you stand regarding each type of skill. Are your skills solid in a specific area or do you need to work on them? Since transferable skills can be used on any job, let's take an assessment to see where you stand as far as they are concerned. These skills should not be listed on your resume or CV, but are important for you to know so that you can brand yourself appropriately for the job or career you want.

GENERAL SKILLS		
SKILLS	STRONG SKILL	NEXT JOB
Meeting deadlines		
Problem solving		
Supervising others		
Accepting responsibility		
Planning		
Controlling budgets		
Efficiency		
Teaching others		
Negotiation		
Organizing/managing projects		
Writing well		

USING HANDS		
SKILLS	STRONG SKILL	NEXT JOB
Assembling things		
Building things		
Repairing things		
Observing/inspecting		

DEALING WITH DATA		
SKILLS	STRONG SKILL	NEXT JOB
Analyzing data		
Auditing records		
Setting up budgets		
Calculating/computing		
Checking for accuracy		
Classification		
Comparing		
Compiling		
Evaluating		
Investigating		
Financial record keeping		
Locating answers/information		
Taking inventory		

USING WORDS AND IDEAS		
SKILLS	STRONG SKILL	NEXT JOB
Articulation		
Inventiveness		
Verbal communication		
Creating new ideas		
Design		
Editing		
Ingenuity		
Logic		
Remembering information		
Writing clearly		
Public speaking		

WORKING WITH PEOPLE		
SKILLS	STRONG SKILL	NEXT JOB
Administration		
Caring for others		
Confronting others		
Being outgoing		
Counseling people		
Persuasion		
Demonstration		
Being pleasant		
Being diplomatic		
Sensitivity		
Being sociable		
Helping others		
Insightfulness		
Tact		
Tolerance		
Toughness		
Interviewing people		
Kindness		
Listening		
Mentoring others		
Trusting		
Understanding		

LEADERSHIP		
SKILLS	STRONG SKILL	NEXT JOB
Arranging social functions		
Initiating new tasks		
Competition		
Decisiveness		
Delegation		
Running meetings		
Self confidence		
Making decisions		
Mediation		

CREATIVITY/ARTISTRY		
SKILLS	STRONG SKILL	NEXT JOB
Artistry		
Drawing		
Painting		
Expression		
Performing/acting		
Presenting artistic idea		
Dance/body movement		
Singing		
Playing an instrument		

Using your results from the assessment, list your top five transferable skills

1. _____
2. _____
3. _____
4. _____
5. _____

Can you see yourself using your identified transferable skills in your future career? (circle your response):   **Yes   No**

Let's recap, what does completing all of these assessments have to do with you finding a future job/career? First of all, the assessment tools help you to learn more about yourself and your personality. This information will be useful in the future for many aspects of the job search. When asked questions about yourself during the interview process, your assessment results will enable you to respond in a way that will be understood by the person interviewing you. After determining your skills, the next step is to set goals toward achieving the career of your dreams.

PART 2
DEVELOP

Setting Goals For Your Future Career

Why Set Goals?

Goal setting is used by successful people in all fields. Setting goals gives you long-term vision and short-term motivation. It focuses your acquisition of knowledge, and helps you to organize your time and your resources so that you can make the most of your life. Goal setting is particularly useful when searching for your career. By setting sharp, clearly defined goals, you can measure and take pride in the achievement of those goals, and most importantly you will be able to see forward progress in what might previously have been an otherwise tedious job search. You will also raise your self-confidence, as you recognize your own ability and competence in achieving the goals that you've set.

SMART Goal Setting

To get started you need first to understand how to set SMART goals. Setting SMART goals will help your goals to be more powerful. There are plenty of variants for each letter of the acronym, but SMART usually stands for:

S - Specific

The goal should state the exact level of performance expected and detail the outcomes criteria. To set specific goals, include dates, times, and amounts so that you can gauge achievement. If you do this, you'll know exactly when you have achieved the goal, and can take complete satisfaction from having achieved it in the time you specified.

M - Measurable

Setting measurable goals allows you to to achieve objectives and then to observe and measure the progress.

A - Achievable

Base your goals on your own personal performance, then you can keep control over the achievement of your goals, and draw satisfaction from reaching them.

R - Realistic
It's important to set goals that you can achieve and that are reasonable. Be sure to set realistic goals for yourself.

T - Timely
Always include specific timeframes so that you can stay on course to meet your goals.

When setting goals for your career, start with the larger SMART goal and work backwards. For example, your overall long term goal could be to obtain a position as a rocket scientist in a Fortune 500 company in Georgia by the end of next year (you should state the actual year). The more specific you are the better. Now let's examine this goal to see if it's a SMART goal:

- **Is It Specific?**
  Yes, exactly what you want to achieve is stated. (Rocket Scientist, Fortune 500 company, Georgia).
- **Is It Measurable?**
  Yes, (in a Fortune 500 company)
- **Is It Achievable?**
  Yes, if you have everything you need to do so and you can get started doing what is necessary. (The necessities can be addressed in your short term goals).
- **Is It Realistic?**
  Yes, once again we need to be sure that for any career that you are considering, you are qualified already for the position or are working toward becoming qualified, this can be addressed in your short term goals as well.
- **Is It Timely?**
  Yes, (by the end of next year).

This is a suitable and SMART long term goal. The next step is to write the supporting short term goals to ensure that your long term goal can actually be met. Once your SMART goals are all written you can start working on achieving them. Practice creating long and short term SMART goals for one year, six months, and one month of progressively smaller goals that support your overall one year goal of finding your career position. Next create a daily To-Do List of things you should do today to work toward your career goal. THIS STEP IS SO IMPORTANT! When starting out, your short term goals might be to determine your interests and gather information to take steps toward obtaining the position you want to fulfill your ultimate long term career goal. So far you have been working on this by reading and completing the activities in this book. So you are already on the right path. Finally review your plans, and make sure that they fit the way in which you want to live your life.

When you've achieved a goal, take the time to enjoy the satisfaction of having done so. Absorb the implications of the goal achievement, and observe the progress you have made toward other goals. "One of the biggest tips that I give people who are goal-setting is to celebrate those small wins. People want the end result, but again, you have to keep in mind the timeline. Those small victories along the way should be absolutely celebrated, recognized, and compounded. You want to keep doing the same thing that has gotten you results" (Fowler citing Khalfani-Cox, 2022). Setting up a reward system for yourself when you meet your goals can serve as an incentive to keep striving toward reaching your goals. If you learn something that will make it easier for you to reach future goals, implement it. If you notice a deficit in your skills despite achieving the goal, decide whether to set goals to supplement your deficiencies or rewrite the goal entirely. Remember that failing to meet goals doesn't matter as much as learning something from the experience that will make it easier next time. Incorporate any lessons you learn back into your goal setting process. Remember that goals can change even while you are working on them. Adjust them regularly to reflect growth in your knowledge and experience, and if your goals no longer appeal to you, let them go and rewrite more suitable goals.

GOAL SETTING EXAMPLE

For her New Year's Resolution, Taylor has decided to think about what she really wants to do with her life. Her SMART long term goals are as follows:

■ **Career Goal**

"To be managing editor of X magazine, where I am currently working, by June of 20XX."

■ **Artistic Goal**

"To keep working on my illustration skills by spending time drawing every day for 2 hours starting today, November 1, 20XX until December 31, 20XX. Ultimately I want to have my own show in our downtown gallery."

■ **Physical Goal**

"To run the Boston marathon which is scheduled for May 15, 20XX."

Now that Taylor has listed her long term goals, she then breaks down each one into smaller, more manageable goals. Let's take a closer look at how she might break down her long term career goal - to become managing editor of her magazine:

■ **Five-Year Goal**

"Become deputy editor."

■ **One-Year Goal**

"Volunteer for at least 7 projects that the current Managing Editor is heading up."

■ **Six-Month Goal**

"Go back to school and finish my journalism degree this semester. The semester starts on January 10, 20XX.

■ **One-Month Goal**

"Talk to the current managing editor to determine what skills are needed to do the job."

When talking to the managing editor you might say, "Your job looks interesting to me. One day I might want to be a managing editor somewhere. Can you tell me about your daily tasks and your career path?"

■ **One-Week Goal**

"Schedule a meeting with the managing editor."

As you can see from this example, breaking big goals down into smaller, more manageable goals makes it far easier to see how the goal will get accomplished.

Remember that goal setting is an important method of:
1. Deciding what you want to achieve in your life.
2. Separating what's important from what's irrelevant, or a distraction.

3. Motivating yourself.
4. Building your self-confidence, based upon successful achievement of your set goals.

Set your long term goals first. Then, set a plan of smaller goals that you need to complete if you are to reach your overall career plan. The timing of your goals is up to you. Keep the process going by regularly reviewing and updating your goals. And remember to take time to enjoy the satisfaction of achieving your goals when you do so. Remember to make SMART goals: specific, measurable, achievable, realistic and timely!

Start right now to set your goals. As you make this technique a part of your life, you'll find your career accelerating, and you'll wonder how you ever did anything without setting SMART goals. To help you set SMART goals, below is a list of words to use:

SUGGESTED WORDS TO USE WHEN WRITING SMART GOALS

- **Choose a Verb**
  to increase, to decrease, to reduce, to prove, to deliver, to grow
- **Define the Object**
  what you wish or will work toward to get better at and for whom
- **Identify How Much**
  focus on your target goals and how you will know you have met them
- **Identify by When**
  time frame for completion of goal

STAYING ON COURSE

Once you've decided on your first set of long term and short term (supporting) goals, keep the process going by reviewing and updating your To-Do List on a daily basis. Periodically review your longer term goals, and modify them to reflect your changing priorities and experiences. A good way to do this is to schedule regular assessment sessions to review and update your goals using a journal or computer spreadsheet.

You've set your SMART goals. Now let's work on identifying your values. Knowing your values is a very important part of getting to know yourself and developing your brand.

Identify Your Top Five Values

Go through the list of values below. Eliminate words that don't apply to you and put a check mark next to the values that are important to you.

Accessibility	Stability	Recognition	Learning
Courage	Adventure	Teamwork	Respect
Empathy	Determination	Ambition	Winning
Honesty	Expertise	Compassion	Calmness
Originality	Independence	Family	Directness
Speed	Power	Kindness	Generosity
Accomplishment	Strength	Relaxation	Love
Creativity	Affection	Understanding	Security
Enthusiasm	Clarity	Assertiveness	Celebrity
Humor	Fairness	Completion	Discipline
Passion	Integrity	Fidelity	Grace
Spirituality	Prosperity	Knowledge	Loyalty
Accountability	Success	Reliability	Sensitivity
Curiosity	Affluence	Vision	Challenge
Excellence	Comfort	Balance	Diversity
Imagination	Faith	Contentment	Growth
Peace	Intelligence	Flexibility	Mindfulness
Spontaneity	Punctuality	Leadership	Significance
Accuracy	Sympathy	Resourcefulness	Charity
Dependability	Altruism	Wealth	Efficiency
Experience	Commitment	Bravery	Health
Impact	Fame	Control	Optimism
Perfection	Justice	Fun	Sincerity

Based on the values you selected, answer the following questions:

- Are you living in alignment with your top five values?
- Are you building your life and living authentically?
- Can you see this value in your day-to-day interactions?

If the answer to any of these questions is no, then you need to make adjustments. Your values and activities must be compatible in order for you to move forward authentically.

Identify Your Strengths and Talents

Another step that is important in establishing your brand is to find out what your areas of strengths or talents are. Using the following CliftonStrengths assessment, find out what your areas of strength are and what your talents are and how your individual talents associate with specific careers.

CLIFTONSTRENGTHS ASSESSMENT

The CliftonStrengths Assessment measures the intensity of your talents in each of the 34 CliftonStrengths themes. These 34 themes represent what people do best. Based on Gallup's 40-year study of human strengths, the Clifton StrengthsFinder Assessment was created to help people discover and describe their talents or areas of strength. Once an individual discovers their talents, these talents can be further examined to determine how their assessment results can help them move toward their purpose from a position of strength rather than weakness. Because CliftonStrengths focuses on the greatest opportunities for personal development and success (rather than on areas of weaknesses), you can use your assessment results to focus on what you do best and tackle things like finding your career job (Clifton, 2017).

CLIFTON STRENGTHSFINDER™ THEMES

The Clifton StrengthsFinder™ measures the presence of 34 talent themes. Talents are people's naturally recurring patterns of thought, feeling, or behavior that impact a person's behavior and performance.

Read each description and rate yourself in each theme on a scale of 1-10, 10 being the highest. Review to find your top 5.

TALENT THEME	DESCRIPTION	SCORE 1-10
Achiever	People strong in the Achiever theme have a great deal of stamina and work hard. They take great satisfaction from being busy and productive.	
Activator	People strong in the Activator theme can make things happen by turning thoughts into action. They are often impatient.	
Adaptability	People strong in the Adaptability theme prefer to "go with the flow." They tend to be "now" people who take things as they come and discover the future one day at a time.	
Analytical	People strong in the Analytical theme search for reasons and causes. They have the ability to think about all the factors that might affect a situation.	
Arranger	People strong in the Arranger theme can organize, but they also have a flexibility that complements this ability. They like to figure out how all the pieces and resources can be arranged for maximum productivity.	
Belief	People strong in the Belief theme have certain core values that are unchanging. Out of these values emerges a defined purpose for their life.	
Command	People strong in the Command theme have presence. They can take control of a situation and make decisions.	
Communication	People strong in the Communication theme generally find it easy to put their thoughts into words. They are good conversationalists and presenters.	
Competition	People strong in the Competition theme measure their progress against the performance of others. They strive to win first place and revel in contests.	
Connectedness	People strong in the Connectedness theme have faith in the links between all things. They believe there are few coincidences and that almost every event has a reason.	
Consistency	People strong in the Consistency there are keenly aware of the need to treat people the same. They try to treat everyone in the world fairly by setting up clear rules and adhering to them.	
Context	People strong in the Context theme enjoy thinking about the past. They understand the present by researching its history.	
Deliberate	People strong in the Deliberative theme are best described by the serious care they take in making decisions or choices. They anticipate the obstacles.	
Developer	People strong in the Developer theme recognize and cultivate the potential in others. They spot the signs of each small improvement and derive satisfaction from these improvements.	

TALENT THEME	DESCRIPTION	SCORE 1-10
Discipline	People strong in the Discipline theme enjoy routine and structure. Their world is best described by the order they create.	
Fairness/Empathy	People strong in the Fairness/Empathy theme can sense the feelings of other people by imagining themselves in others' lives or others' situations.	
Focus™	People strong in the Focus theme can take a direction, follow through, and make the corrections necessary to stay on track. They prioritize, then act.	
Futuristic	People strong in the Futuristic theme are inspired by the future and what could be. They inspire others with their visions of the future.	
Harmony	People strong in the Harmony theme look for consensus. They don't enjoy conflict; rather, they seek areas of agreement.	
Ideation	People strong in the Ideation theme are fascinated by ideas. They are able to find connections between seemingly disparate phenomena.	
Inclusiveness/Includer	People strong in the Inclusiveness/Includer theme are accepting of others. They show awareness of those who feel left out, and make an effort to include them.	
Individualization	People strong in the Individualization theme are intrigued with the unique qualities of each person. They have a gift for figuring out how people who are different can work together productively.	
Input	People strong in the input theme have a craving to know more. Often they like to collect and archive all kinds of information.	
Intellection	People strong in the Intellection theme are characterized by their intellectual activity. They are introspective and appreciate intellectual discussions.	
Learner	People strong in the Learner theme have a great desire to learn and want to continuously improve. In particular, the process of learning, rather than the outcome, excites them.	
Maximizer	People strong in the Maximizer theme focus on strengths as a way to stimulate personal and group excellence. They seek to transform something strong into something superb.	
Positivity	People strong in the Positivity theme have an enthusiasm that is contagious. They are upbeat and can get others excited about what they are going to do.	
Relator	People who are strong in the Relator theme enjoy close relationships with others. They find deep satisfaction in working hard with friends to achieve a goal.	
Responsibility	People strong in the Responsibility theme take psychological ownership of what they say they will do. They are committed to stable values such as honesty and loyalty.	

TALENT THEME	DESCRIPTION	SCORE 1-10
Restorative	People strong in the Restorative theme are adept at dealing with problems. They are good at figuring out what is wrong and resolving it.	
Self-Assurance	People strong in the Self-Assurance theme feel confident in their ability to manage their own lives. They possess an inner compass that gives them confidence that their decisions are right.	
Significance	People strong in the Significance theme want to be very important in the eyes of others. They are independent and want to be recognized.	
Strategic™	People strong in the Strategic theme create alternative ways to proceed. Faced with any given scenario they can quickly spot the relevant patterns and issues.	
Woo	People strong in the Woo theme love the challenge of meeting new people and winning them over. They derive satisfaction from breaking the ice and making a connection with another person.	

Adapted from Discover Your CliftonStrengths (Clifton, 2017)

My Top 5 CliftonStrengths Themes Are:

1. _____
2. _____
3. _____
4. _____
5. _____

Developing Your Brand

Now that you have completed the Clifton's StrengthsFinder Assessment and determined your top themes, you will need to use all the information you have learned previously from the other assessments you have completed in this book to begin to personally brand yourself for your new career. The information you have gained about yourself as a result of completing the assessments will aid you in forming the foundation of your personal brand and can help you determine how to move forward to reach your career goals (Dugan, 2019).

There is no way around it. Since the job market has shifted so rapidly, in order to land a career job today you have to brand yourself. You must become the employee that the hiring manager is seeking and you have to distinguish yourself as the "product" of choice.

If you think about it, branding is nothing new. It's all around us and has been relevant as far back as we can remember. Many studies have been done which have revealed that young children can identify brands at earlier ages. Entire libraries of books have been written about the importance of branding and every entrepreneur or seller of goods and services realizes the importance of branding their products or services in a way that will make the customer remember and ultimately purchase their offerings time and time again. This idea is not so different from the concept of personal branding. Except now the brand is you. You have to brand yourself in such a way to be the only choice for the employer to consider. In order to do this you have to thoroughly know yourself and be able to anticipate what the hiring manager needs to be successful in their company. It takes a bit of guesswork and also requires that you really know the job market in which you are searching. In addition it requires that you have the skills and qualifications necessary to get the job done. If you are interested in trying something new you will need to brand yourself as a self starter and a go getter who can and will quickly be able to hit the ground running to be able to accommodate the needs of the hiring manager.

We know that personal branding is the practice of people marketing themselves and their skills and abilities as brands. It also involves the creation of self as an asset by defining skills, abilities, image, and attire in a way that leads to making a memorable impression on potential employers and is the ongoing process of establishing a prescribed image or impression in the mind of others which will lead to securing the job over the competitors (Dugan, 2019).

Additionally, here are a few tips from an article written by Mary Eileen Willliams, *5 Amazing Ways to Brand Yourself for Job Success*, to further describe the importance of personal branding to the job search process:

■ As a job-seeker, this means you'll need to ensure that all of your written materials are eye-catching and pleasing to read. Incorporate liberal use of bullets and white space on your resume, in your cover letters, in each of your online profiles (LinkedIn) and on all employment documents.

■ Whenever you're out and about meeting people, at networking events and, most especially, at a job interview, dress the part. Attire and grooming actually do matter.

■ Watch your nonverbal messages. Be sure that your mannerisms exude confidence, warmth, enthusiasm and energy.

■ Employers who will potentially "buy" you represent your customer base; target your elevator pitch or message to meet their needs.

■ You can determine which keywords are in the greatest demand by using the online job postings as your primary research tool. Review them carefully and identify the skills that are requested over and over again. Again, while you won't need to list your skills, you will need to have examples that can show the hiring manager what gains you have made in the past or will be able to make in the future that showcases your skills. On job postings, note the order in which any requirements are placed. This way, you'll gain both an accurate reading of skills that are currently in demand and the order of their value to employers.

■ Communicate demonstrated ways you will outperform the competition. In order to set yourself apart from your competitors, you'll need to sell your distinguishing features to the hiring manager through your resume, cover letter and personal communication.

■ Emphasize the added value you will bring as a uniquely qualified individual. What makes you better/more qualified than other candidates? Which talents, attributes and skills differentiate you from the competition? What experiences have provided you with a unique perspective on your work?

- Develop your Elevator Pitch which should clearly show how you can make an exceptional contribution to the goals of your potential employer.

- Obtain referrals from trusted sources.

- Alert your network to the positions/organizations you are targeting and let them know how they can support your efforts.

- Provide your contacts with a copy of your resume so they're aware of how you are presenting yourself and which accomplishments you're highlighting.

- Be certain to prepare each of your references so that they can best recommend you for a particular opportunity.

- Know your real value in the marketplace. Determine the income range you will feel comfortable accepting. Check out sites such as Salary.com and Glassdoor.com to ascertain what similar positions are paying.

- Develop an adaptable approach to negotiating salary and benefits. Although you'll want to be paid fairly for your skills and experience, your ultimate goal is to create a win/win situation with your new employer.

The above information is adapted from Wake Tech Personal Branding Course, citing the work of Mary Eileen Williams.

Also please note, you will need to adapt your resume and branding statement or summary profile to each job/career that you are interested in. Since we believe the information that you discovered in the assessments is accurate, the way in which you adapt yourself will be based on the truth. The point of personally branding yourself to each position is simple-you want to present your best self to the hiring manager. You want to be exactly what they are looking for, the individual who is the best fit for the position at hand based upon your attributes, experience, and proven ability to excel in the position. You need to be the answer to whatever issue they are facing in their organization.

PART 3
PREPARE

Resume Building

When you create a brand that centers on your professional goals, accomplishments and skills, you can better identify new opportunities to advance and develop. Written elements of your personal brand can serve as a reminder of your objectives as you search for a job, craft your resume and cover letter or prepare for an interview. You may also discover opportunities that you want to pursue that you hadn't previously considered. Make sure you include elements of your branding into your employability documents (resumes, cover letters) to make sure that your brand message is present and consistent throughout your materials.

TYPES OF RESUMES

There are many types of resumes that you can use in your employment search. Of the various types of resumes that exist, chronological, combination, functional, etc. you will need to choose a type that is compatible with your brand and that showcases what you have done in your past positions that portrays you in the best light. Remember that your resume should support the brand that you have developed. You will need to incorporate a branding statement or if your resume will be submitted electronically, a summary profile/professional summary, that separates you from your competitors at the top of your resume. And your resume, regardless of the format, should be written in reverse chronological order, listing your most recent jobs first. Adapt your resume so that it shows your quantifiable accomplishments in your past positions rather than just listing skills. Showcase your wins. Do not list skills or job duties but rather list how your being at a particular company benefited that company. Adapt your resume and branding statement or summary profile to fit your needs, communicate your brand, and show your prospective employer why you are exactly the employee they are looking for.

Next comes your Branding Statement. Remember this statement will need to be tweaked depending on the position you are seeking. You may and definitely should have several resumes but certain aspects of each will be the same though since your overall brand should represent you generally, regardless of the job you are seeking.

Following the Branding Statement, list your work experience in reverse chronological order, starting with the job you had most recently. Include dates in the month/year format, i.e. 10/202X - 03/202X. There is no need to include dates within the month. If you have gaps in employment, be willing and able to discuss them. Always be truthful on your resume, applications and in your interviews.

In the section where you list your past positions, include a general description of what you did in the position to set yourself aside from your peers. Choose your points wisely and include quantifiable gains that you made for the organizations where you worked previously. This is where you sell yourself and highlight your gains!

When preparing your resume for electronic submission to match a particular job posting, check out the actual posting and use as many of the keywords that you see in the posting as you can without going overboard. This is for the benefit of applicant tracking software (this will be explained later). Emphasize your accomplishments that speak to what the hiring manager needs most. Remember you are the answer to what the hiring manager is seeking, you have what it takes, now use your past accolades and gains to make sure that you stand out and shine!

Now let's concentrate on actually creating your branding statement. But first, let's review, what is a branding statement?

Simply put, a branding statement is a short statement highlighting your most relevant expertise in about 15 words or less. You should place the branding statement at the top of your resume to explain, first and foremost, what you can bring to an employer. The branding statement is a brief synopsis, however, you can elaborate further on your key qualifications through a longer summary statement or in person at the interview (Doyle, 2020).

WHAT TO INCLUDE IN YOUR BRANDING STATEMENT

A strong branding statement conveys exceptional qualities, skills, experiences, or areas of knowledge that will distinguish you from the average candidate. Branding statements should be tailored toward a particular job and show how you have the qualifications to excel in that position.

To start drafting your branding statement:

■ Take an inventory of your accomplishments in your most relevant employment experiences.
■ Make note of the personal assets which you drew upon to generate those successes.
■ Analyze the requirements of the job you are seeking and look for any overlap between what you've done in the past and what is needed by the new hiring manager.
■ Select three or four adjectives that describe your key strengths. Weave together the adjectives with your desired job title or role and tie them to the value-added.
■ Write it all down in a short statement. That's it! Once you have completed a branding statement make sure to place it on your resume right below your contact information and before the Experience section of your resume (Doyle, 2020).

EXAMPLE:

Jane Doe
E: jane.doe@email.com
C: 555-555-5555
LinkedIn: http://www.linkedin.com/pub/jane-doe/8e217b431

Creative, skilled, social media expert with five years of experience managing more than 100 professional social media accounts of a large corporation.

Professional Experience
Social Media and Marketing Manager, ABC PR Company, Silver Springs, MD
March 2021-Present

SUMMARY PROFILE

According to Columbia University Center for Career Education (n.d.), a resume summary or summary profile, as we refer to it in this book, is a brief statement at the top of your resume that highlights your accomplishments and skills. It's purpose is to show the employer why you're qualified for the job! Much like a branding statement, a summary profile when used now and in the past, is important and serves in lieu of a branding statement. Depending on how your resume is submitted and the particular job you're seeking, you may want to have a resume on hand that features a summary profile rather than a branding statement. If you choose to incorporate a summary profile section on your resume make sure that it is powerful.

To get started,

■ Research positions of interest and write a list of the common requirements and qualifications. Some things that you will want to make note of are: the size and number of employees, major products and services the company provides, who the competitors of the company are, reputation and values of the company, history of the company. You will also need to make note of the name of the interviewer or hiring manager, how many people will be conducting the interview, the type of interview, main duties and responsibilities of the position and salary range of the position or other similar positions in your geographic area.

■ Assess your skills and credentials. Determine how your background and experience aligns with the qualifications outlined in the job description? Review your skills, experiences, special knowledge, and accomplishments that you want to highlight in the summary profile selection.

■ Next draft a few phrases that summarize your Skills/Experience/Accomplishments/Knowledge/Education but be careful to not just provide a laundry list of line items. Instead pull out keywords from the job description and connect your experiences to those keywords in the event that your resume is being electronically submitted using applicant tracking system technology.

APPLICANT TRACKING SYSTEMS

The applicant tracking system (ATS) is a method that many employers use to screen and eliminate resumes for many jobs today where employment documents are electronically submitted. Basically it means that your resume doesn't go to a human being after submission, but to a computer. The ATS software is designed to scan resumes for certain keywords, skills and job titles and to weed out the ones that don't match the keywords found in the associated job description.

So, if you want your resume to actually make it into the hands of a human being, you need to make sure it's optimized for ATS. Once resumes are scanned, those that pass the test are sorted and then moved along for consideration. The other resumes are not considered. Hiring managers can then screen candidates who submitted resumes that matched based on keywords that were identified as a match based on the ATS, as well as track their progress through the hiring process. By digitizing the hiring process in this way, an ATS saves employers time and money.

For example, if a recruiter is hiring for an Office Assistant position and there are 300 resumes, the first step initiated by the ATS system would likely be to search for "Office Assistant." This step would isolate candidates that have done the exact job before from those who have not. Anyone that doesn't have that exact term on their resume would not be considered.

A search can also contain multiple terms. For example, recruiters might perform a complex search that contains a combination of job titles and skills: Office Assistant AND data entry AND payroll to further sort applicants. This information can be useful to applicants who have scanned the job postings for which they are applying for keywords, job titles and skills. If they can include the keywords found in the job description in their resume, they will have a greater chance of being considered than those who don't include keywords in their application materials (Henderson, 2022).

In conclusion, after preparing your resume make sure your resume:
- Includes your contact information at the very top (your name, your email, your

LinkedIn profile URL and your telephone number). If you don't have a LinkedIn profile, now is the time to create one.
- Is error free. Solicit several proofreaders to ensure that your resume is error free.
- Contains a professional email address
- Does not contain false or exaggerated statements
- Has a font size that is appropriate for easy reading
- Is specific to the job you are pursuing
- Is short; one page is best.

Developing Your Elevator Pitch

For face-to-face interactions, an elevator pitch is a quick way of introducing yourself to another person that tells who you are, what you do, what skills you have that set you apart, and offers an invitation to have a further discussion by telling how you can be contacted, setting up a follow up discussion immediately or asking for an opportunity to collaborate with the individual you are addressing. Additionally, elevator pitches are particularly useful to answer the "Tell me a little about yourself" question when interviewing for a job, when meeting with people that you might want to conduct business or collaborate with in some way, or when marketing goods and services.

Elevator pitches are personal to you and it is important that they be genuine, accurately delivered, clear and concise. The idea is to make the idea of an interview, a meeting or a collaboration exciting and mutually beneficial. Elevator pitches are quick verbal messages and really should be no longer than one minute. When originally created, the idea was to be able to pitch yourself to another person in the time that it took for an elevator to go from one floor to another. Since the pitches should be short and concise, you will need to pay attention to include specific things in your pitch. Having a good elevator pitch can help you to refine your brand and prepare you to be ready to use it when the time is right. Use the following steps to create your elevator pitch, as outlined by Jennifer Herrity of Indeed (2022).

HOW TO CREATE THE PERFECT ELEVATOR PITCH

■ Introduce Yourself
Make sure to introduce yourself using your first and last name. Point out any association you have with a company or organization, or how you found out about the person you are talking with.

■ Explain What You Do
In one or two sentences explain what you do and the specific problem you have experience solving (pain point). If you are selling a product, quickly introduce it and tell how it will solve a problem that exists in society or a pain point that your client is experiencing. If you're seeking a job, quickly discuss your professional abilities, areas of expertise, and quantifiable impacts you have made for a company or industry you were previously associated with.

■ Identify Who You Serve
In one or two sentences explain who you consider your audience to be. Reiterate how you or your product can be helpful to your audience. If you're a job candidate or seeking an interview, consider discussing why you want to work for the hiring company with whom the person you are speaking with is associated.

■ Include An Exciting Hook Or Create Excitement
Add a hook at the end of your pitch that is memorable and which gains the attention of the person you are pitching. For example to capture the attention of your audience, include how your product or service can impact their lives. You could also use a thought-provoking question instead of a statement, such as one that addresses the problem that they may be experiencing.

■ Using The Steps In The Items Above, Create A Cohesive Pitch
Make sure that it is conversational and natural. Practice your elevator pitch aloud and try it out on a few friends to be sure that it is understandable and conveys what you want to communicate.

ELEVATOR PITCH EXAMPLE

Review the elevator pitch below to guide you in writing your own.

Elevator pitch for marketing a new travel app idea:
Do you like to travel? If yes, do you ever wish there was a way to input all of the travel information into an app to help you find your way in a new place including restaurants, modes of transportation, navigation, language, restaurants, hotels and everything you will possibly need to be able to experience your trip with ease? My name is Selena May, and I'm a software designer. I've built My Travel Guide, an app that allows users to upload links, images, notes, maps and more for different destinations, even abroad. My app allows travelers, or even just people who appreciate their hometowns or new destinations with a way to explore new places easily and even helps when traveling abroad! In preliminary testing, 96% of users said this app improved their travel experience and saved them time and money by eliminating all guesswork in the travel experience. When can we get together so I can tell you more about My Travel Guide?

Now it's your turn to create your own elevator pitch using the 5 steps provided above. Write out all of the portions of your elevator pitch on the lines below and then rearrange the information in a concise and logical way. At the very end, ask for a meeting or if you can speak further with them about how you can collaborate, find out about the job opportunity, or ask for a meeting to determine next steps.
Your Elevator Pitch

1. Introduce yourself

_____
_____
_____
_____

2. Explain what you do (if marketing a product, include how it will solve their pain point)

_____
_____
_____
_____

3. Identify who you serve

_____
_____
_____
_____

4. Include an exciting hook or create excitement.

_____
_____
_____
_____

5. Now put it all together (remember to ask for a meeting, interview, etc)!

_____
_____
_____
_____

After completing your Elevator Pitch practice in front of a mirror saying it over and over until it becomes second nature. Practice it in front of your friends and ask for their feedback. Make sure that you sound confident and that you convey what makes you the right person for the position or why the person to whom you are speaking should want to talk with you further.

To recap, as mentioned previously, in the past the traditional job search method was the way to go for anyone seeking a new job. It worked well and there was really no reason to question its validity. Today and in recent years, we have seen a shift in the job market and in the ways in which new opportunities are sought. Traditional methods to search for jobs can work for some people as well as work well in some career fields, but are not as reliable as they once were. Therefore, new and different methods need to be developed and utilized in order for today's job seekers to be able to stand out among their peers. As a new entrepreneur I found myself facing similar challenges. I asked myself and others the question, "What am I able to say or do that those with similar businesses cannot?" In seeking answers to this question, I was told by master entrepreneurs that I would have to communicate to my target audience how I am the absolute best at what I do, and how the services I provide are undoubtedly the answer to any problem they may have.

The same way of thinking is applicable to the job search process. As a prospective employee you must determine how you can use the skills you have and/or skills you can readily obtain to solve any pain that your prospective employer has or can potentially have. You literally have to be a problem solver and a pain stopper for your prospective employer. The first steps, however, have already been outlined in the earlier chapters of this book. They are to know your interests, yourself, personality, values, and skills. This understanding can help you personally brand yourself and position yourself to be the answer, solution, and key to success for your employer and, ultimately, for yourself. Then you must use whatever method you can to get in front of your prospective employer and communicate your worth! Beforehand, you should prepare an elevator pitch, network in person and through social media platforms, ask connections to introduce you, etc. Then make the magic happen by being prepared to communicate what you have done in the past and what skills you possess that would make you the obvious candidate, the only candidate. Don't prepare a scripted laundry list of accolades to spout off to the hiring manager, instead discuss examples of what you have done in the past and can do immediately that can be utilized by your hiring manager to eliminate his or her pain and move the organization forward.

In this book we are discussing new routes to get to the same end goal – a great job or career. But you can also still use the old ways of the traditional job search in addition to what you are learning here. In your quest, you will want to research jobs online and elsewhere that are interesting to you. Make sure you are passionate about these jobs that are on your shortlist and that you have the necessary skills to obtain them. Have variations of your resumes with your branding statement or summary profile ready. Having several versions of your resume will serve you well. When you are able to personally discuss your resume, use a branding statement and when you are submitting your resume online use a summary profile filled with keywords from the job description that can be recognized by the applicant tracking systems that are in place in many organizations.

In either case regardless of which version of resume you are using, to find out more about jobs, research the Internet, research companies that employ people who you feel are working in your career field, check out the LinkedIn profiles of these people, connect with and conduct informational interviews with connections on LinkedIn to find out more about what they do on a daily basis, check online job search engines and read and study the job descriptions to see if you have what it takes to pursue a career that matches the careers on which you are focusing.

Your Employment Search: Stand Out Through Your Personal Brand

The personal brand experience benefits both you and the prospective employer. According to brand expert, William Arruda, as stated at Forbes.com, "your personal brand is your most valuable career asset. It is absolutely essential" (Arruda, 2022). It is your opportunity to learn more about yourself so that you can identify your unique skills, strengths and talents. "It's a celebration of you and your individuality and the value that you will deliver while working each day" (Arruda, 2022). It's your chance to tap into your values and passions to find your purpose. Your personal brand should be a reflection of you.

Refining your brand will help you to:
- Know who you are
- Know your values
- Know your skills and what you have to offer the employer
- Know what makes your way of doing things unique, interesting or different
- Know your strengths
- Network and build an online image through Linkedin and other social media sites
- Develop a professional image
- Perfect your attire
- Be able to sell yourself – create your elevator pitch

Next, spend some time thinking about what makes you different from your peers – your strengths, your passions, your values, and your goals. Ask yourself, "If you left your job today, what would your company and colleagues miss?" Know who you are, as well as who you are not.

One of the best ways to articulate your skills, experience, knowledge, and overall worth in today's competitive job market is to create a personal brand that helps you stand out in the crowd. According to management expert and author Tom Peters, "We are CEOs of our own companies: Me Inc. To be in business today, our most important job is to be head marketer of a brand called You." Everything you do ultimately contributes to your personal brand.

Once your brand has been defined, make sure that the little things – the way you dress, your body language, how you behave with others, the emails you write – are consistent with your brand message. Update your resume to reflect your values, brand

and what you bring to the process for the betterment of your prospective employer. Analyze your resume to determine if it truly represents your brand, accurately defines who you are, and is in line with both your short-term and long-term goals.

Set up accounts at social networking sites such as Linkedin, Facebook and Twitter. Market yourself constantly and provide updates on a daily basis. Make sure your updates to social media and your employment documents are germane to your branding message.

The above is adapted from *Sell Yourself: 14 Steps to Creating a Powerful Personal Brand* by Dawn Dugan, Salary.com contributing writer.

Building Your Network

WHERE TO NETWORK

Where should you network? Good question. You might think that you should network broadly because you are searching for your career and you will need all the help you can possibly get. This may be true but you really want to be strategic about where and with whom you network. First of all, what is networking? According to the New Oxford American Dictionary (2022), networking is described as the action or process of interacting with others to exchange information and develop professional or social contacts: "the skills of networking, bargaining, and negotiation." Remember, networking is not the process of making cold calls or connecting with people who you don't know for the sake of increasing your social media numbers. It's all about personal connection and it is a reciprocal process.

Now that you know what networking is, you need to learn how to strategically network to find the career that you are searching for. Once you have found an area of career interest, you will want to begin networking. While researching, find a few organizations that support your career interests. Though we are focusing on networking as a great way to make connections with individuals that can aid you in your job search, please do not forget to take advantage of some of the more traditional methods that can help you get a job as well such as, job boards/postings, employment agencies, job/career fairs, classified ads, career services departments on your university campus or job placement offices. Check LinkedIn for any connections you may have that work at the organizations you have chosen. If you are not on LinkedIn, you will need to build your own profile at this time. Once you have any connections on LinkedIn in your field of interest, contact them and ask if you can speak to them briefly about their experience at the organization that you are interested in working for. Make sure to be courteous and not overbearing. Find professional associations that support your interests. You can also research any professional organization on LinkedIn as well as elsewhere on the Internet. Pay particular attention to the mission, vision statements, culture, and values of organizations you are interested in working for and professional associations that support your career choice. Thoroughly check out their webpages. Make sure that your values align with each before going any further in the networking process.

Once you have found a few, let's say 3-4 potential employers, you can think about how best to market yourself to them. Think about what you can contribute to any organization, based on your past work experience, that will alleviate problems or pain points for them. This will be your hook. If you find that the hiring manager of an organization is trying to solve a particular problem, figure out how you can help solve the issue should you be offered employment there. You already should have figured out your skill set so you will need to compare your current skill set with what will be needed to solve any issue that the prospective employer is faced with. If you don't have the necessary skills to help, get training or figure out a way to become knowledgeable in that specific area. If you cannot do this, then you need to abandon the search with this particular organization and continue your research. Tailor your resume and elevator pitch to what is needed by any organization that you have on your radar. Become comfortable discussing how, if you are hired, you will be able to help the organization. It's much easier to target 3-4 organizations and to conduct research on a few of them rather than to send out dozens of resumes, cover letters/E-cover letters or conduct informational interviews. Remember that you will have to keep track of everything that you are doing to attract the attention of every organization so a targeted, limited search is best. You can also network in many other places such as at professional conferences, trade shows, conventions, and networking events, among colleagues you've worked with and through professional organizations you belong to. You may also want to reach out to past employers as well. Researching websites such as firsthand.co and legacy.vault.com can be helpful as well, as you search for your new position. Networking is an ongoing process. It really doesn't ever need to stop. Remember, networking is a two-way street. All parties should benefit from the relationship! Don't ever walk away from a networking opportunity without asking how you can assist the person you're asking for help.

USING LINKEDIN FOR NETWORKING

LinkedIn is a social networking site that was developed in 2002. Its main purpose is to help people and businesses network professionally. LinkedIn is free for basic service. There is a fee associated with its premium service but you can use it for free on a trial basis once you have begun to actively search. LinkedIn allows you to find and connect with others through the site and by using it properly you can connect with both known and unknown business associates, clients, and colleagues. Additionally, LinkedIn can be used for career development and allows those seeking a job to post their resumes, curriculum vitae (CV) and interests and allows employers to post and recruit for positions they are trying to fill in their organizations.

Once you have connected with someone on LinkedIn, you then have access to all their connections. These connections ultimately become your extended network. You can ask your primary connections to introduce you to their connections, allowing you to access others whom you would never have had access to.

In making connections on LinkedIn remember that you are initially building a mutually beneficial relationship with your potential connection. In your initial contact make sure to contact the person directly, be concise, point out areas of commonality, such as "I recognize you from the annual meeting of the XYZ Corporation which was held last June. May I add you to my professional network?" Sending a personal message such as this will help to establish rapport between you and your potential connection.

DEFINITIONS THAT WILL HELP YOU TO UNDERSTAND LINKEDIN
- **Connections:** registered users who you know personally.
- **Second-degree connections:** the connections that your connections have who may be known or unknown to you.
- **Third-degree connections:** any connections from your second-degree connections.
- **Profile page:** your personal information page. Contains all of your important information that you would like to be displayed regarding your education, work history, publications, activities and so on. Your LinkedIn profile should tell your audience 1) Who are you and who you help, 2) Why you are passionate about what you do, 3) What is unique about you, 4) How the current opportunity relates to your goals and aspirations and 5) How you'd like to hear from them.
- **Recommendations:** you can ask your former employers or connections to write recommendations for you, which will be displayed on your LinkedIn profile page.

LinkedIn can be used professionally for networking purposes as mentioned previously. It can also be used for communicating with your connections and for conducting research on specific people and organizations that you would like to know more about, be employed by, or with whom you would like to conduct business.

LinkedIn is a great option for job hunting. You can use LinkedIn to conduct preliminary research about an employer and about people who are associated with a particular organization. You can find out a great deal about an organization's culture, policies and values by using LinkedIn as well as the organization's website.

ORGANIZING YOUR NETWORKING AND JOB SEARCH
Use forms like the following example to organize your search. Create a database or utilize some system to keep yourself organized. Record all interviews, calls, or

appointments by the name of the company, date, and time. Keep track of the resumes and cover letters that you send by date and job title. Determine the best methods to follow up and ask about the job status. Keep notes on the job status including who you spoke to when following up. If you don't get the job, you may want to ask for pointers to help on your next interview or ask for specific tips regarding how to improve your interview skills.

NETWORKING ORGANIZER				
NAME	ADDRESS/EMAIL	TELEPHONE	DATE(S) OF CONTACT	NOTES

Setting up your Job Search Tracking System

So far you have been performing a lot of tasks to help you to understand yourself better. By understanding yourself better you can present yourself to those you are trying to impress. This is also the time for you to set up a system to track your efforts. Once the interviews start you will want to keep track of the companies you have contacted, the hiring manager's name, dates of the contact or interview, dates by which to follow up and other important information pertaining to the positions. It is so important that you organize yourself so that you can be on top of your searches.

There are many ways in which you can organize your searches. Just remember, this is an important step that you must be sure to take in order to make the most of your time and efforts. You might want to create a database or spreadsheet to keep track of everything, or you might want to use file folders. Regardless of what you do to keep track, please keep track of what is going on with your search.

You will also want to have several versions of your resume or curriculum vitae (CV) handy and also various cover letters that can be adapted for each position that you apply for.

DAILY PLAN PREPARATION

Finding a job/career is a job! I know you have heard this before. You should spend a specific amount of time daily looking for opportunities. As you are working daily, keep track of who you are contacting, what you are sending them, and how you plan to follow up by date. Each day, as you continue to search for opportunities, be sure to check to see if you are due to follow up with a person or company that you contacted previously. Some of the items you might want to include on your follow up sheets are: current date, company name, how you found out about the position; whether by word of mouth or website, or job posting, position title, pertinent information about the position/company, telephone number of the company, your expectations, if you have submitted anything and to whom, and a follow-up date.

Regardless of where or how you are looking for your new job or career, you will need to be organized in your search.

MONTHLY PLAN PREPARATION

At the end of the month, make sure to check everything that you have been updating daily regarding your search. If positions have been filled or they are no longer of interest, record that the position is no longer an option and add the date as well.

Filling Out Applications

At some point during your career search you may have to fill out an application. Applications are often needed for entry level positions, and the information on them can serve as an introduction to the hiring manager. If an application is needed for a position for which you are applying, remember these tips to make sure that your application reflects that you are the best candidate for the job.

- Read the entire application before filling out any information.
- Use a blue or black ink pen or a computer.
- Complete all sections. If you find that a section does not apply, write "N/A" for "not applicable" to indicate that the information does not apply to you and that you did not forget to answer the question.
- Be as neat as possible. If you make an error, cross out the incorrect information with a single line or neatly use correction tape (don't overuse correction tape).
- Answer the questions honestly.
- List a specific position for which you are applying.
- If you are asked to indicate a salary, input a range. If you are not allowed to put a range of figures, input a salary within the range that you determined based upon your research.
- Proofread your application before submitting.
- Take your time to fill out the application accurately.
- Have your resume on hand as well as contact information for any references.
- Follow up on your job application by contacting the hiring manager or a contact in Human Resources. Give a call after two to three days unless you have been told otherwise at the time of submission.

The Interview Process

An interview assists employers in screening applicants to fill vacancies within their organization. There are many types of interviews which we will discuss in the paragraphs that follow. The interview is often the first contact between an employer and a prospective employee, therefore it is important that candidates properly prepare for them and are able to make a great first impression to be invited for a second interview and perhaps even a third. In order to prepare for an interview, an applicant should be ready mentally and physically.

In today's society phone or video interviews are becoming more common as a way to save time and money for an organization. Therefore, it is a good idea to practice participating in these types of interviews as well as in traditional interviews. First let's discuss the types of interviews you may have to face in a typical job search.

Types of Interviews

SCREENING INTERVIEW
A phone or video interview is a very cost effective way to screen candidates.
A screening interview usually is a great way for an employer to determine if they want to pursue a prospective employee for candidacy. These types of interviews typically last about 10 to 45 minutes.
When you are scheduled for a screening or telephone interview, have your resume, the job description, a list of references, prepared answers to challenging questions, a few questions that you have written that you can ask the interviewer, and brief information about the company nearby. Have a mirror on the wall or nearby so that you can remember to smile and be aware of your facial expressions during the interview.

ZOOM OR OTHER VIDEO INTERVIEW

Recently, more than ever, video interviews are being conducted on Zoom, Skype, Teams, Meet or other platforms. When participating on these platforms make sure that you have the appropriate app downloaded to your computer, tablet or device before the video starts.

Tips that you should keep in mind are as follows:

- Dress in interview attire for the interview even if it is being conducted by video. Your mindset will be different if you are interviewing in pajamas!
- Prepare for the interview in the same way you would for an in-person interview.
- Make sure your answers are succinct and to the point.
- Make sure your device is fully charged and that the Internet connection is strong.
- Do not use filters or backgrounds of any kind during your interview. Make sure that the interviewer is able to hear you clearly by asking if your volume is sufficient.
- Make sure that the area where you are interviewing is well lit, quiet and free from distractions. (no babies, kids, or pets)
- Be on time to accept or make the video call.
- Have a contact phone number for the hiring manager just in case something unexpected happens and the video call is interrupted in some way.
- Be aware of body language. Sit up straight in the chair and relax. Use eye contact and be energetic. Be careful of excessive gesturing, which can be seen on camera.
- Be sure to ask what the next step in the interview process will be.

ONE-ON-ONE INTERVIEW (IN-PERSON)

This is the most common type of interview. These interviews typically range from 30 to 60 minutes for most positions and are usually held at the job site.

Tips to keep in mind for one-on-one interviews:

- It is okay to think for a bit of time before beginning to answer the question.
- It is okay to ask for the question to be rephrased.
- Make eye contact with the interviewer.
- Try to establish rapport with the interviewer. Research your interviewers so you can mention things you might have in common.

GROUP, PANEL OR COMMITTEE INTERVIEW

These interviews usually consist of three or more interviewers who take turns asking questions of the prospective candidate. Research all interviewers so you can mention things you might have in common.

Tips to keep in mind for group, panel or committee interviews:
- Greet and shake everyone's hand before and after the interview.
- The purpose of the interview is that it serves as an efficient way to interview one candidate and obtain each group member's interpretation of a candidate's answers from various perspectives.

POTENTIAL WAYS TO DESCRIBE YOURSELF

Ambitious:	A strong wish to be successful.
Conscientious:	Wishing to do what is right, thorough
Determined:	To make a firm decision to do something.
Honest:	Truthful and willing to not lie, steal, or cheat anyone.
Mature:	Behaving in a sensible, adult way.
Optimistic:	Always believe that things will turn out successfully or for the best.
Organized:	To arrange things neatly and in order.
Outgoing:	Very sociable and friendly.
Perfectionist:	A person who has high standards, exacting
Persistent:	To keep doing something in spite of obstacles
Polite:	Having good manners, being well-behaved and courteous to others.
Responsible:	Can be trusted to do something.
Self-Motivated:	The ability or willingness to take a first step in doing something.
Tactful:	To be sensitive and not hurt anyone when handling a situation.
Well-Spoken:	To talk or say words well.
Willing:	Ready and eager to offer help or do what is asked.

INTERVIEW CHECKLIST

Use the checklist below to prepare for each interview you secure. If you can answer Yes to the following questions, you are well-prepared.

YES	NO	INTERVIEW CHECKLIST
		I have researched the company thoroughly.
		I can discuss ways in which I can make a difference in the company to improve their processes, functions, sales, productivity, etc.
		I can clearly explain what makes me different from my competitors based upon my expertise and/or experience.
		I have the names and information of all individuals who will be interviewing me.
		I have the training, education, experiences and skills that qualify me for the job or I am in the process of obtaining them.
		I have the contact and information of at least 3 references that I can provide.
		I have researched the company culture and have prepared my attire appropriately.
		(For an in-person interview) I have directions to the company and plan to arrive at least 15 minutes early.
		(For Online interview) I have made sure that my computer is functioning and that I have Internet connectivity.
		I have all necessary documents with me in preparation for the interview.
		I have prepared two to three questions to ask the interviewer.

SAMPLE INTERVIEW QUESTIONS TO ASK

You should have at least two to three questions prepared to ask the interviewer. One of the questions should be relevant to next steps in the interview process. This question will help you to follow up appropriately to the initial interview.

Your follow up questions should be well thought out in advance and can include questions about job performance, climate of the organization, pressures of the job, skill requirements, educational requirements, work demands, the hiring process, or any other topic relevant to the position.

Some questions to consider are below:

- In what department would a person with my skills usually work?
- What kind of person does well in your organization?
- In which ways can the company improve?
- What are the three biggest problems current employees say they are experiencing?
- What is your stance on experience vs. education as a qualification?
- What is the timeline for filling this position?
- When can I expect to hear from you next?
- Do you have any uncertainty about me that I can clear up?
- What specific qualities will make the new hire indispensable to the team?

PART 4
PRESENT

Preparing for your interview also involves anticipating what some of the interview questions might be. Take the time to research common interview questions online and practice answering these questions! Look for an opportunity during the interview to specifically tell the hiring manager how you will be able to solve any problems that are occurring at the organization based upon your personal branding and the research you have already done about the company that you are interviewing with or the industry in general. Answering questions that benefit the employer and the organization is a way to set yourself apart from your peers and put you on the short list to be considered for hire.

In preparation for your interview, respond to the following questions and prompts in as much detail as you can. Your answers should relate to your resume, your LinkedIn profile, and the job posting.

1. Personality traits or skills I have that are job related:

_____
_____
_____
_____
_____

2. Examples of experiences I have had that demonstrate the above traits/skills and quantifiable wins that I have achieved:

_____
_____
_____
_____
_____

3. 3-5 accomplishments that would be of interest to the person interviewing me:

_____
_____
_____
_____
_____

4. What are the 3 most important things I want the interviewer to know about me?

_____
_____

5. What concerns might an employer have about me and what will alleviate those concerns?

6. What specifically have I done or what experience do I have that can demonstrate how I solved a particular issue for my past employer? Do you have any experiences that affected the bottom line of the organization? In other words what problem did you solve or have the ability to solve? How can you use your past experiences, skills and knowledge to alleviate pain for the interviewer and is your experience quantifiable? (think long and hard about this one!)

ROADSIDE NOTES

When I was growing up I never had a job outside the home. No McDonald's or anything. If I needed money I asked my parents and they figured it out somehow. Once I went away to college I was told I didn't have to work because my parents, my mom especially, wanted me to be able to concentrate on my studies and not to be worried about working. I found jobs on campus anyway because I was trying to relieve some of their financial burden in whatever way I could.

When I came home for the summer I worked at the factory where my father worked alongside some of his colleagues who also had their teens working for the summer. My father was not the most talkative person but one day he said to me, "come on, get ready you are going to work with me today." Now I hadn't told him I was interested in working for the summer and I didn't know that other workers had made arrangements for their teens to work there either. All I know is that when my father said "come on, get ready," I got up and got ready. I also didn't know anything about the job and wrongfully assumed that I'd be working in the front office because after all, I was a college student majoring in business education and I could perform office administrative tasks very well. Furthermore, I was going to teach these same subjects to students upon graduation. I dressed up for my first day and thought, *this is so cool. I don't even have to interview for a great summer job working in an office.* I put on a nice blazer, skirt, blouse and heels and I was ready for work. I got in the car and my father drove us to work. Now if you will remember, I told you my father worked in a factory. The factory manufactured cotton goods. People working there wore jeans, t-shirts, and thick soled shoes to protect themselves from standing and working on the concrete floor for hours.

So, long story short, I showed up dressed completely wrong. You can imagine my surprise and the surprise of the other employees who were there. Everyone stared at me in disbelief and my father didn't say one word. The next day and for three summers following, I followed the advice that a nice lady named Mary told me on that first day: "Tomorrow, wear some jeans and a t-shirt, socks and some shoes that will allow you to stand and work on concrete." This also taught me a lesson about researching the job responsibilities before showing up!

ATTIRE - DRESSING FOR THE INTERVIEW

What's the best outfit to wear to a job interview? The answer will vary depending on the type of job and company you're interviewing with. You always want to dress to make the best impression, but the outfit you choose depends on where you are interviewing. Dressing appropriately is important because the first judgment an interviewer makes is going to be based on how you look and what you are wearing (DeLeon, 2021).

In general you will want to wear what is considered professional, or business attire for an interview. For men, this would mean a suit jacket and pants, shirt and tie. For women, you might want to wear a blouse and pants, a pantsuit or skirt suit. To avoid distractions in either case you should remember that less is more. Nothing that you are wearing as an accessory should take the attention away from the main outfit. When preparing your interview outfit, keep in mind that it is better to be neat, clean and somewhat conservatively dressed than distracting and over-the-top. You may want to stay with solid, darker colors and consider a pop of color rather than anything that is flashy. Before choosing your interview attire, be sure to research the company and find out what the employees that currently work there wear. It makes no sense to dress in a t-shirt and jeans for an interview in a business office, or to dress in a nice shirt, tie, and dress pants for a job at a loading dock. However, you should look professional and neat regardless of the type of position for which you are interviewing.

If you are interviewing for a job in an informal work setting, you will want to interview in an outfit that falls into the business casual category. Business casual calls for an outfit that falls between the professional expectation of a business suit, button-down shirt and tie and the casual attire of a t-shirt and jeans. A button-down shirt and khaki pants with a belt could be an option for men. If you are not sure of what the proper attire to wear for your interview, make a call to the receptionist or the person who scheduled your interview to ask for help.

If you are interviewing for your first professional job after college or going for a job directly from high school, dress professionally and be sure to behave in a professional manner once you are hired. Nobody needs to know this is your first professional job. Wow them with your ability to rise to any occasion.

If you are a college student, be sure to dress professionally when interviewing for a professional job or internship. These opportunities will guide you in how to properly dress for interviews in the future. In general, regarding accessories, hair, make-up and perfume or cologne, remember less is more. You do not want to overwhelm the interviewer in any area. Err on the side of caution and tone down anything that can distract from the reason you are there – to get the offer.

FOLLOWING UP AFTER THE INTERVIEW

It's important to follow up after the interview. In these changing times I believe courtesy always wins out. In order to follow up you need to do your research before the interview occurs. Make sure that you have the names of those involved in the hiring process at your disposal along with their contact information. Sending an email or even a handwritten note is a nice gesture that can set you apart. Additionally, at the end of the interview one of the questions that you should ask is what are the next steps in the hiring process? It's a great question to ask and will allow you to have an expectation of when you could possibly hear from them next. In your (error free!) follow-up note or email, you can also re-emphasize your interest in the position, inform them of something you forgot to mention, and let them know that they can contact you with further questions. If you are in a group interview, you should send a note or email to every person involved in the group. You may also follow up within a week to ten days of the interview with a telephone call to ask about the status of the position unless you have received other information from the hiring manager at the end of the initial interview.

FINDING A MENTOR

Finding mentors that can help you navigate your way on your job is extremely important. You can find mentors easily by finding someone to emulate who has been on a path similar to the one that you are now on. Stay in contact with your mentors because the information that they will share with you is invaluable. Also realize that as you go through experiences in your career, others may wish for you to mentor them. You have something to offer others as well. Learn from your experiences and then share the information you learn with others who are coming behind you. Associating yourself with others who are new to the organization or with those who have experienced a similar path is a great goal to have.

JOINING PROFESSIONAL ORGANIZATIONS

In order to keep abreast of the latest knowledge and practices of a particular industry you might want to join a professional organization. This is also a great way to show dedication to the field in which you would like to work. By being a member of professional organizations you can learn more about the industry in which you will be working and you can find mentors as well. As a member of a professional organization you will also be able to take advantage of professional development, networking opportunities, education and have a chance to enhance your business profile.

PART 5
PREVAIL

The Job Offer

When the hiring manager has determined you are the right person for the job you will be presented with a job offer which will include a letter of agreement. A job offer is an invitation to work for an employer that is presented to a prospective employee (Zippia, 2022). An offer can be informal (offer and a handshake) or formal (a written letter or email outlining the specifics of the position). It is best to receive an offer in writing to have a written record of the offer, but an informal offer is still acceptable. Once a prospective employee receives an offer it must be accepted by a letter of acceptance being sent by the prospective employee or verbally in order for the employee to be officially hired. Before accepting the offer, is the time to negotiate the offer items if you are not comfortable with them. Once a final agreement has been reached between the hiring manager and the prospective employee regarding the terms of the offer, employment can be finalized.

Job offers usually contain information about the scope of your employment, such as:
- Job title and position
- Start date of employment
- Salary
- Benefits
- Reporting structure
- Location of employment
- Other terms and conditions

NEGOTIATION SKILLS

After you have received a job offer you will need to determine if you should negotiate it. I would recommend that you do so since most employers have a salary range from which they are operating and may not offer you the top salary in the initial offer. In order to prepare yourself for the negotiation process, make sure that you have already researched the salary range for the position online on Glassdoor.com, Google, or other websites regarding similar positions within your geographic area. This will give you an idea if the salary offer that you received seems fair. You can then ask for a salary at the top of the range. The hiring manager might accept your request or may counter. If the salary that you are offered is lower than you expected, take a look at the benefits offered. Remember the benefits are a valuable part of your compensation package. In today's market, benefits can make up 32 percent of an employee's total compensation (Woodruff, 2020). However, benefits can vary by the size of the organization, industry group and geographic location. You can negotiate these items also. Benefits that may be negotiable include: (PTO) paid time off, start date, vacation time, sick leave, remote work, sign on bonus, professional development opportunities, yearly bonus, stock options, employee discounts, tuition reimbursement, additional leave, daycare reimbursement, office space, guaranteed severance package, phone allowance, retirement benefits matching, transportation benefits, moving expenses, travel benefits, job title, cost of living adjustments, preferred parking, profit sharing, and flexible work schedule. Keep in mind that although you may certainly attempt to negotiate your offer, sometimes it will not result in your favor. Reasons why your counter offer may not be accepted could possibly be because the organization has made the best offer they are willing to make due to budget constraints, you are underqualified or you have been underemployed and the organization is unwilling to make any adjustment, or your offer is beyond what other employees are making. After you receive information about the total offer if you are still dissatisfied but you want the job, you might want to ask for an earlier performance review than usual with an option to re-discuss. Once an agreement has been made between the hiring manager and the prospective employee and the offer has been accepted, it's official.

Showing Up Authentically

Be yourself at work. Understand your boundaries and respect the boundaries of others. Communicate effectively with your co-workers on all levels and if any issues arise work to solve them in a diplomatic way. Being authentic is not always easy but it is always the right thing to do. Being true to yourself can help others to follow suit. Celebrate your successes and if you make a mistake, make it right. Authenticity makes for a more cohesive and comfortable workplace for everyone.

WORKPLACE ETIQUETTE

Workplace etiquette is important because it creates a professional, mutually respectful atmosphere and improves communication, which helps an organization and its workers serve as a productive place. People feel better about their jobs when they feel respected, and that translates into better customer relationships as well.

When starting your new position, be courteous and respectful to your coworkers. Establish a rapport with your boss and co-workers that is friendly yet respectful. Take notes regarding the things that you are being told regarding your job so that you can avoid asking for help later. Take your cues from the other employees who should be setting examples for you. Make sure that you adhere to the office attire by dressing appropriately. Arrive to work and leave on time. Find and suggest ways to improve the work environment if you can but always be courteous when suggesting changes. Always be professional and adopt a "you" attitude–consider others' needs and the company's feelings first. This behavior leads to good manners and common courtesy, thereby improving your workplace etiquette (GCF Global, n.d.).

Conclusion

The purpose of this book was to help you, the job seeker, accomplish a few tasks which would allow you to know yourself better, set SMART goals, determine your strengths, interests, personality traits, your values and what you value, your career interests, and then utilize this information to be able to look deep inside and formulate a strategy to brand yourself and ultimately sell yourself as a top choice worth considering for the employment opportunities which you are seeking. The end result of your exploration would allow you to be able to position yourself as the answer to the problems your potential employer is facing and actually be able to use your past accomplishments as a springboard to become the choice candidate in a sea of others.

If you followed this introspective path to personal discovery, I am sure you found out some information that will be useful in understanding who you are and why you are the way you are. These personal discoveries will enable you to formulate a personal brand and elevator pitch that can be used to position yourself as the answer to any pain points the hiring manager might have. Armed with this information you are well on your way to landing a position that you are passionate about and that allows you to use the many attributes you possess in your new career. You have what it takes and you are well capable of reaching your career goals. Let's go!

Glossary

ACCOMPLISHMENTS – These are the achievements you have had in your career, especially ones that you can quantify.

APPLICANT TRACKING SYSTEMS (ATS) – A method used by some employers to collect, store job candidate data and screen resumes from potential job candidates.

ASSESSMENTS – These tests ask you a series of questions and try to provide you with some sense of your personality and career interests. The results of assessments can be a good starting point for discovering more about yourself and your interests and considering careers you may not have contemplated.

BENEFITS – An important part of a compensation package, and part of the salary negotiation process. These benefits may include paid vacations, company holidays, personal days, sick leave, life insurance, medical insurance, retirement and pension plans, tuition assistance, child care, stock options, and more.

BRANDING STATEMENT – A statement placed at the top of a job-seeker's resume that tells immediately what he/she can bring to an employer.

CAREER BRANDING/BRANDING – Helps define who the applicant is and why they should be hired. Branding is a promise of an applicant's value to an employer and showcases what sets them apart from other job seekers.

CAREER CHANGE – Changing occupation by devising a strategy to find new career choices. Most experts now predict that the average person will change careers three to five times over the course of his or her work life.

CAREER EXPLORATION – The process of finding a rewarding career path, as well as specific jobs within a particular career path.

CAREER PLANNING – The continuous process of evaluating your current lifestyle, likes/dislikes, passions, skills, personality, dream job, and current job and career path and making corrections and improvements to better prepare for future steps in your career, as needed, or to make a career change.

CLASSIFIED AD – an advertisement in a newspaper or magazine, generally dealing with offers of or requests for a job.

CLIFTONSTRENGTHS – An assessment that measures the presence of 34 talent themes. Talents are people's naturally recurring patterns of thought, feeling, or behavior that impact a person's behavior and performance.

COMPENSATION PACKAGE – The combination of salary and fringe benefits an employer provides to an employee. When evaluating competing job offers, a job-seeker should consider the total package and not just salary. See also **salary and benefits**.

CORPORATE CULTURE – The collection of beliefs, expectations, and values shared by an organization's members and transmitted from one generation of employees to another. The culture sets norms (rules of conduct) that define acceptable behavior of employees of the organization.

COUNTER OFFER/COUNTER PROPOSAL – A salary negotiation technique used by job-seekers when a job offer is not at an acceptable level. Almost all elements of a job offer are negotiable, including the salary, non-salary compensation, moving expenses, benefits, and job-specific issues.

COVER LETTER – A cover letter accompanies your resume and opens a window to your personality (and describes specific strengths and skills you offer the employer). It should entice the employer to read your resume.

> ■ **cold contact cover letter** – The most common type of cover letter, since 80-95 percent of the job market is "closed," meaning the job openings are not advertised. Usually part of a direct mail campaign in which the job-seeker is trying to uncover hidden jobs.

■ **cover letter** – An extremely effective type of cover letter that springs from networking efforts. The referral letter uses a name-dropping tactic as early as possible in the letter to attract the reader's attention and prompt an interview.

CURRICULUM VITAE (CV) – See **resume**.

ELECTRONIC RESUME (OR E-RESUME) – A resume that is sent to the employer electronically to be scanned or searched by optical scanning systems, either via email, or by submitting to Internet job boards.

ELEVATOR PITCH (OR ELEVATOR SPEECH) – A 15- to 30-second commercial that job-seekers use in a variety of situations (career fairs, networking events, job interviews, cold calling) that succinctly tells the person you are giving it to who you are, what makes you unique, and the benefits you can provide.

EMAIL COVER LETTER – A cover letter (see **cover letter**) that is sent to the employer electronically via email discussing your experience and interest in a potential job.

EMPLOYMENT AGENCY – an organization that helps find jobs for persons seeking employment or assists employers in finding persons to fill positions that are available.

EMPLOYMENT GAPS/GAPS – Are those periods of time between jobs when job-seekers are unemployed, either by choice or circumstances. Employers do not like seeing unexplained gaps on resumes, and there are numerous strategies for reducing the impact of these gaps on your future job-hunting.

ENTREPRENEUR – Someone who starts and runs his or her own business.

FOLLOW-UP – A critical part of job-hunting which consists of contacting employers after you've submitted a resume and are waiting to hear from the hiring manager. Follow-up is also important after the job interview, by sending a thank-you letter and an email expressing your interest and fit for the position.

FUNCTIONAL RESUME – See **resume**.

HOLLAND CODES – Personality types developed by psychologist John L. Holland as part of his theory of career choice. Holland mapped these types into a hexagon which he then broke down into the RIASEC job environments (see RIASEC). See also **assessments**.

INFORMATIONAL INTERVIEWING – The process of a prospective employee spending time with a network contact in a highly focused conversation that provides the prospective employee with key information needed to launch or boost a career.

INTERNSHIPS – A way in which a person can gain valuable experience by experiencing direct exposure to the business environment and obtaining valuable references and network contacts.

INTERVIEW – A meeting between a prospective applicant and a hiring manager to determine if the fit is right between them.
- **screening interview** - interview designed to weed out unqualified candidates.
- **traditional interview** - uses broad-based questions such as, "why do you want to work for this company?" and "tell me about your strengths and weaknesses."
- **panel/group interview** - uses a committee of people, usually around a table, asking questions.
- **situational interview** - sometimes also referred to as a scenario-based (problem-solving) interview, where the job-seeker is placed in a hypothetical situation (such as dealing with an irate customer), and is judged by how well s/he reacts to complex information and their ability to resolve problems and arrive at solutions.
- **stress interview** - usually are a deliberate attempt to see how you handle yourself under pressure. The interviewer may be sarcastic or argumentative, or may keep you waiting.
- **phone interview** - a preliminary technique used by employers to decide if

there is a good enough match to justify a site visit.

JOB APPLICATION – An application for employment at a particular organization.

JOB BOARD – a website or physical board located within an organization which is used by employers to advertise their job vacancies to job seekers. Some well-known internet job board sites are Indeed, Glassdoor, and Careerjet.

JOB FAIR – See **career fair**.

JOB OFFER – See **offer of employment**.

JOB PLACEMENT OFFICE – a service for finding a job for a job seeker.

JOB POSTING – See **job board**.

JOB SHADOWING – A work-based learning activity that provides job-seekers with opportunities to gather information on a wide variety of career possibilities before deciding where they want to focus their attention. Job shadows involve brief visits to a variety of workplaces, during which time you "shadow," observe, and ask questions of individual workers.

JOB SKILLS – The skills you need to perform a particular job. For example, an accountant needs to have good math and accounting skills; a doctor needs to have good medical, scientific, and personal skills.

LETTER OF ACCEPTANCE – Used to confirm the offer of employment and the conditions of the offer; i.e., salary, benefits, starting employment date, etc. It is always a good idea to get the entire offer in writing.

LETTER OF AGREEMENT – A brief letter outlining the conditions of employment.

LETTER OF RECOMMENDATION – A letter of support for your skills, ability, and work ethic, usually written by a former boss or co-worker, but could also be from a teacher or personal reference.

MENTOR – A person at a higher level within a company who counsels or guides another less experienced mentee in their career.

MENTORSHIP – relationship in which a more experienced or more knowledgeable person helps to guide a less experienced or less knowledgeable person,

MYERS-BRIGGS – Based on typological theories originated by Carl Jung, the Myers-Briggs Type Indicator (MBTI) assessment is a psychometric questionnaire designed to measure psychological preferences in how people perceive the world and make decisions. The original developers of the personality inventory were Katharine Cook Briggs and her daughter, Isabel Briggs Myers. The 16 different types are usually referred to by an abbreviation of four letters. One of each of the following pairs constitutes one's four-letter type: Extraversion or Introversion, Sensing or iNtuition, Thinking or Feeling, and Judging or Perceiving. See also Assessments. Find assessments using this method.

NETWORKING – Involves developing a broad list of contacts through various social, professional, and business functions, and soliciting their support when searching for a job.

NON-VERBAL COMMUNICATION – How you present yourself in an interview. Includes activities such as handshake, eye contact, facial expressions (including smiling), body posture, and hand gestures.

OCCUPATIONAL OUTLOOK HANDBOOK – Published by the U.S. Department of Labor, Bureau of Labor Statistics, this guide provides detailed information on more than 250 occupations. The Handbook discusses the nature of the work and the typical working conditions for persons in each occupation. In addition, it details the requirements for entry and the opportunities for advancement.

OFFER OF EMPLOYMENT – An offer by an employer to a prospective employee that usually specifies the terms of an employment arrangement, including starting date, salary, benefits, working conditions.

PERSONAL BRANDING – See **career branding**.

PROFESSIONAL SUMMARY – (see **summary profile**) a resume summary which sits at the very top of your resume and is your first chance to make a great impression with a hiring manager.

QUESTIONS – Toward the end of most job interviews, the interviewer will give the job-seeker an opportunity to ask questions. Doing so shows your interest in the position and employer.

RECRUITERS/HEADHUNTERS/EXECUTIVE SEARCH FIRMS – Professionals who are paid by employers to find candidates for specific positions. They often recruit candidates, but job-seekers can also approach them.

REFERENCE LIST – Sometimes also referred to as a **reference sheet**. Simply a listing with key contact information of your references.

REFERENCES – A group of people who will say good things about you and who know specific strengths that you offer. Can include work references (current and past supervisors), educational references (former teachers or school administrators), and personal references (who can speak of your character).

RESEARCHING COMPANIES – The process of gathering information about a company, its products, its locations, its corporate culture, its financial successes. This information is extremely valuable in a job interview where you can show off your knowledge of the company, and can also help you in writing your cover letter.

RESUME – A key job-hunting tool used to get an interview to find out more about the company and present yourself as a viable job candidate, it summarizes your accomplishments, your education, as well as your work experience, and should reflect your usefulness to your past employers based upon your job performance "wins."

- **chronological resume** - the most common type of job-seeker resume, it's a resume organized by your employment history in reverse chronological order, with company/job titles/accomplishments/dates of employment.
- **functional resumes** - a resume organized by skills and functions; bare-bones employment history often listed as a separate section.
- **keyword resumes** - an e-resume typically identified by a keyword summary (and heavy usage of keywords throughout the resume) that emphasizes key nouns and phrases.
- **scannable resumes** - a resume that has been prepared to maximize the job seeker's visibility in an electronic resume database or electronic resume tracking system. Becoming somewhat less important as more and more companies simply request electronic versions of resumes.
- **text resumes** - also referred to as text-based or ASCII resumes, a resume that has been prepared to maximize the job seeker's visibility in an electronic resume database or electronic resume tracking system.
- **video resumes** - a video resume is a short video of the job-seeker essentially selling himself or herself to potential employers. Contrary to its name, a video resume is not your resume on video but actually a short promo enticing the employer to take a look at your "real" resume.
- **web-based resume** - a resume that resides on the Web. A Web-based resume can range from quite ordinary to very elaborate. Fundamental principles of good resume writing, content, and design apply.
- **curriculum vitae** - also called a CV or vita and similar to a resume, but more formal, and includes a detailed listing of items beyond the typical resume items, such as publications, presentations, professional activities, honors, and additional information. Tends to be used by international job-seekers, and those seeking a faculty, research, clinical, or scientific position.

RIASEC - Acronym for the career-related personality types developed by psychologist John L. Holland. The letters in RIASEC stand for: Realistic (practical, physical, hands-on, tool-oriented); Investigative (analytical, intellectual, scientific, explorative); Artistic (creative, original, independent, chaotic); Social (cooperative, supporting, helping, healing/nurturing); Enterprising (competitive environments, leadership, persuading); Conventional (detail-oriented, organizing, clerical). See also **assessments**.

SALARY - Financial compensation an employee receives for performing the job, and part of your compensation package. Can be determined by hourly, daily, weekly, monthly, and yearly.

SALARY HISTORY - A salary history tells a prospective employer the level and frequency of your promotions and full compensation that was received in each job.

SALARY NEGOTIATION - An important process in which job-seekers attempt to obtain the best compensation package possible, based on skills and experience, the industry salary range, and the company's guidelines. See also **benefits**, **compensation package**, and **salary**.

SALARY REQUIREMENTS - The expected compensation for a position. The best strategy is to state that you are "open" to any fair offer and are willing to negotiate but have a range in mind based upon your research.

SCREENING INTERVIEW - an interview is designed to weed out unqualified candidates.

SUMMARY PROFILE - (see professional summary) a resume summary sits at the very top of your resume and is your first chance to make a great impression with a hiring manager.

THANK YOU LETTER - A letter sent which should be sent after every interview thanking each person who participated in the interview process.

TRANSFERABLE SKILLS - A list of skills acquired during life activities and through jobs, classes, projects, parenting, hobbies, and other life experiences. These skills can be transferred from job to job.

UNDEREMPLOYED - A person who is not working full-time at a level that matches his or her education, experience, and other qualifications. Someone who is working part-time, but seeks full-time employment; or, someone who is working in a lower-level position that requires less experience or skills (thus making the person overqualified for the position).

UNDERQUALIFIED - The underqualified label most often plagues new graduates with limited experience, as well as career-changers whose experience is outside the area they now wish to pursue.

VOLUNTEERING - Offering your services free of charge, typically to a not-for-profit organization.

Adapted From Quintessential Careers.

ABOUT THE AUTHOR

Dr. Greta Oliver is a professional coach specializing in student development, career development and leadership development devoted to helping those in transition. As evidenced by her 30 years of experience working with and on behalf of students on every educational level and her experience as a corporate training specialist, higher education administrator and adjunct educator in the fields of education and human resource development, she adds her knowledge and career counseling expertise to help those who are transitioning from high school to higher education, those in career transition and those interested in leadership development.

Dr. Oliver is the owner of Greta Oliver Consulting, a hands-on consulting business that specializes in the transition to college, personal development, leadership development, and career training. She is also a best selling author, of her first book in the roadmap series, *College Roadmap: Essential Tips For First Time College Students and Their Families*, and the host of her educational podcast, Educate U.

To find out more, visit
www.GretaOliverConsulting.com

WORKING PAPERS

MY CAREER PLANNING INFORMATION

1. My Holland Code: _____

2. Three careers that interest me based on my Holland Code:
   _____

3. My Myers-Briggs Code: _____

4. Three categories of careers that interest me based upon my Myers Briggs Code:
   _____
   _____

5. My Top Five Transferable Skills:
   _____
   _____

6. My Long Term SMART GOALS:
   _____
   _____

7. My Short Term SMART GOALS:
   _____
   _____

8. My Top Five Values:
   _____
   _____

9. My Top Accomplishments:
   _____
   _____

10. Five Words That Describe Me:
    _____
    _____

NAME	ADDRESS/EMAIL	TELEPHONE	DATE(S) OF CONTACT	NOTES

DATE	EMPLOYER	CONTACT NAME	TELEPHONE	NOTES

DAILY JOB SEARCH LOG

MONTHLY JOB SEARCH LOG				
DATE	EMPLOYER	CONTACT NAME	TELEPHONE	NOTES

REFERENCES

Glossary/Definitions adapted from Quintessential Careers, Dictionary.com and Cambridge.org.

Arruda, W. (2022, October 16). Why You Must Focus on Building Your Personal Brand This Fall. Forbes.com. Retrieved October 16, 2022, from www.forbes.com

DeLeon. (2014, April 27). Attire. HuffPost. Retrieved October 24, 2022, from https://www.huffpost.com/entry/job-search_b_4804394

Doyle, A. (2021, November 11) The Best Interview Attire for Every Type of Interview. Retrieved from https://www.thebalance money.com/best-interview-attire-for-every-type-of-interview-2061364

Doyle, A. (2021) The Best Outfits for Job Interviews. (n.d.). Retrieved from https://www.thebalancemoney.com/best-interview-attire-for-every-type-of-interview-2061

Doyle, A. (Ed.). (2020, December 10). How to Add a Branding Statement to Your Resume. Thebalancemoney.com. Retrieved November 3, 2022.

Dugan, D. (2019, March 18). Brand yourself: 14 steps to creating a powerful personal brand. Salary.com. Retrieved October 29, 2022, from https://www.salary.com/articles/sell-yourself-14-steps-to-creating-a-powerful-personal-brand/

Fowler, B., & Khalfani-Cox, L. (2022, November 14). How to Set Good Financial Goals. LinkedIn.com. Retrieved November 20, 2022

Gallup Press. (2021). StrengthsFinder 2.0 from Gallup: Discover your CliftonStrengths.

GCF Global. (n.d.). Job Success: Business Etiquette - GCF Global . Retrieved January 5, 2023, from https://edu.gcfglobal.org/en/jobsuccess/business-etiquette/1/

Gilman, Cheryl. (2002). Doing Work You Love. Fall River Press.

Gilman, C. (n.d.). Doing Work You Love Now. Retrieved October 5, 2022, from https://www.indeed.com/career-advice/career-development/perfect-elevator-pitch

Harwood, L. (2013). Your Career: How to make it happen. South-Western/Cengage Learning.

Henderson, R. (2022, September 7). What is An ATS? 8 Things You Need to Know About Applicant Tracking Systems. jobscan.co. Retrieved November 22, 2022, from Jobscan.co

Holland Code Assessment from department of workforce services, jobs.utah.gov

Holland Code Type Categories and Descriptions adapted from CareerKey.org

Kolmar, Chris. "Average Number of Jobs in a Lifetime [2022]: All Statistics" Zippia.com. Apr. 5, 2022, https://www.zippia.com/advice/average-number-jobs-in-lifetime

Myers Briggs Personality Assessment Retrieved from http://www.personalitytype.com/career_quizPage3

Nauta, M. M. (2010). The development, evolution, and Status of Holland's theory of Vocational Personalities: Reflections and Future Directions for counseling psychology. Journal of Counseling Psychology, 57(1), 11–22. https://doi.org/10.1037/a0018213

RIASEC Careers List From uManitoba.ca (Note: this list is not all inclusive)

Tiger, P. D., Barron B., and Tieger K. (2014). Do What You Are: Discover the Perfect Career for You Through the Secrets of Personality Type. Little, Brown Spark.

Transferable skills assessment from SkillScan 2021.

Vemparala, T. (2022, November 17). Solving the Mystery of Millennial and Gen Z Job Hoppers. Retrieved December 24, 2022, from https://www.businessnewsdaily.com/7012-millennial-job-hopping.html

Wake Technical Community College (2015, August). Resumes, Branding, Interviews, Employability Skills concepts adapted from the Human Resource Department curriculum.

www.ingramcontent.com/pod-product-compliance
Lightning Source LLC
Chambersburg PA
CBHW071352080526
44587CB00017B/3075